LION OF THE LAKE

BY
LEO MASTERS

One Printers Way
Altona, MB R0G 0B0
Canada

www.friesenpress.com

Copyright © 2024 by Leo Masters
First Edition — 2024

All rights reserved.

No part of this publication may be reproduced in any form, or by any means, electronic or mechanical, including photocopying, recording, or any information browsing, storage, or retrieval system, without permission in writing from FriesenPress.

ISBN
978-1-03-830068-3 (Hardcover)
978-1-03-830067-6 (Paperback)
978-1-03-830069-0 (eBook)

1. BIOGRAPHY & AUTOBIOGRAPHY, PERSONAL MEMOIRS

Distributed to the trade by The Ingram Book Company

Table of Contents

Preface — *vii*

Chapter One: We all must have a beginning. — 1

Chapter Two: The upbringing — 4

Chapter Three: And the high school years begin. — 9

Chapter Four: The college years — 14

Chapter Five: My illustrious life as a career man begins. — 19

Chapter Six: Winter months begin. — 22

Chapter Seven: My career as a resort general manager begins. — 24

Chapter Eight: Freshly groomed and ready to take it all on — 27

Chapter Nine: Tales of the North — 30

Chapter 10: The many wild adventures — 33

Chapter 11: The wild and fun times continue. — 43

Chapter 12: The years that ended bachelor life into engagement — 53

Chapter 13: Marriage and birth of a new child — 58

Chapter 14: The restart of a new life as a bachelor — 73

Chapter 15: Back to where it all started. — 78

Chapter 16: The day that changed my life forever — 86

Final Closing Thoughts — *91*

Preface:

I decided to write this book to tell the stories and journeys of my life.

I have had many adventures that have sculpted and made me into the man I am today. I did not write this to persuade any readers in any direction. I was sitting with some dear friends of mine in the midsummer at the premiere cabin of my family's resort. The father of the family I was visiting happens to be our hometown's most persuasive and powerful attorney (at least in my opinion). He inspired me to write this novel, telling me that, you have a colourful life, dynamic family dramas, with a very well-known business in our area. He went on to tell me that I have a very vivid and comical way of relaying my stories and he had never seen his daughters so attentive to anyone for such a long period of time. My scepticism told me that maybe I went on for too long, but he assured me that I have a lot to tell. I have changed the names of all characters for their privacy and write this for sheer entertainment. The stories are in no order of preference and told to the best of my memories at the time.

CHAPTER ONE:
We all must have a beginning.

I was born in August 1976 in a northern suburb of Chicago, Illinois, called Downers Grove, Westmont. The important part of my August birth date is the birth sign of Leo, thus inspiring the title of this book. This, with the fact that I grew up on the greatest freshwater lake in the world called Lake of the Woods. This lake has over ten thousand islands and sixty thousand miles of shoreline. We have many native art rock paintings and prisoner-of-war-camp remnants from WWII. Some may proclaim it is one of the greatest fishing resources that our planet has to offer. Avid fishermen, having the opportunity in our area, would not argue this fact.

My Father's side of my family has a strong and distinct US Military background. My grandfather retired from the US Air Force as a brigadier general. He set a military record for being the only general who entered as a private and retired with such a high officer ranking. This is no surprise, given the heroic medals he was given. The Purple Heart for swimming to save lives across enemy fire in WW II is his most notable one. He was also a medical doctor with a PhD, which helped him save the lives of wounded comrades in battle.

LION OF THE LAKE

I have an uncle that retired with the US Air Force as a captain after travelling around many parts of the world in service. His young brother is an officer in the Navy Reserves. He attained this from his educational background as a pilot and applying his efforts in submissions through the Navy. My father was sent to St. John's Military High School in Wisconsin where he graduated with honours. I have a cousin that graduated from the Citadel University in South Carolina. This university is famous for its strong military foundation.

My mother was adopted by a Polish family in Chicago. Adopted babies do not get to choose their families but if they did, she could not have asked for a better family to take her in. They are a strong and devoted Polish Catholic family. My grandfather, "Jaja," was a school principal while my grandmother, "Buscha," was a real estate salesperson. This family has a strong medical background with doctors hailing from the Mayo Clinic in Rochester, Minnesota, as well as other fine hospitals throughout the USA.

My father worked for a well-known train company in the northwest part of Chicago. He was an assistant duty manager. He worked there for only a short amount of time, as he dealt with a lot of corruption in this position. Corruption which may have been derived from a famous Mafia family. He convinced my mother to move to Canada, to follow his dream of owning and operating a fishing resort. My grandfather used to take our family to Sioux Narrows, Ontario, Canada, where he purchased a summer cottage. His estate was in the Whitefish Bay area which is known for the cleanest and deepest water on the entire lake. My parents' version of the story is my grandfather helped my father find a full service fishing Lodge so he could purchase this to pursue his dreams. My version is that I was such a prodigy baby at the age of eighteen months that I instantly said, "The city life isn't for me, I am packing my diapers and bottles and heading to Canada." And they agreed to come along.

While I was born in the USA, I have lived most of my life in Canada which now makes me a dual citizen of both countries. My sister and I

Chapter One: We all must have a beginning.

are both truly blessed to have this status from two of the greatest countries in the world. The township of Sioux Narrows had approximately three hundred year-round residents. We grew up in an exceedingly small town, to say the least. My father had every reason to fail at this venture, with no business background or formal education. The resort had also gone bankrupt a few times, with the original owners taking it back each time. They were expecting to have to do the same again. My father had three huge traits in his favour which are will, determination, and a hunger for success. This is where the life I know now began—in Canada.

CHAPTER TWO:
The upbringing

Like anything in life, growing up in a small town had benefits and challenges. One benefit was that we all knew each other, which allowed for quite a bit of trust. Parents felt amazingly comfortable leaving their kids at each other's houses. We had a small curling club with a bar and restaurant in it. The town committee formed a small league—which seemed more like social time at the bar than it did throwing rocks to curl. Curling is an incredibly unique sport to northern countries, where teams of four throw round, flat rocks into a red circle. One person slides a rock while two people sweep with a flat broom and one "skip" yells commands to the sweepers. This game is played on a sheet of ice and in a covered facility. It could be compared to shuffleboard on ice.

Our town was too small for organized sports such as baseball, ice hockey, basketball, and similar popular team sports. We had an outdoor skating rink in the winter as well as cross-country ski trails. I was born in a time before smart phones, laptops, and advanced video games. We learned to make our amusement outdoors with fishing, hunting, snowmobiling, and riding ATVs. It was a great way to grow up, surrounded by clean air, fresh water, wildlife animals, and many kinds of trees

Our town only had one elementary school, from kindergarten to grade six. Our entire school had less than fifty students. My grade had nine students, which seemed exceptionally large in comparison to the

Chapter Two: The upbringing

other smaller-size grades. We had three classrooms. One room was for junior kindergarten and senior kindergarten. Another room held grades one to three while the third held grades four to six. The building also had a small public library. We had three teachers, with one also being the principal. We were very confined, and everyone lived within a mile or two from the school. A small school bus transported us to and from school. In the warm months, I also had the option to bike. And oh boy did I fly like the wind on wheels!

Once grade seven started, we had to take an hour-long bus ride to a town called Kenora. This is a town of approximately sixteen-thousand year-round residents. This district has many summer lake cottages and resorts, growing the population to approximately one hundred thousand in the warm seasons. We commenced into an intermediate school called Lakewood which held grades seven to nine. I felt very overwhelmed as there were approximately five hundred students there and each classroom had twenty to thirty students. Being on the bus for over an hour to get to such a large facility felt like I was getting shipped off to another continent. It seemed that most of the other students knew each other from the Kenora elementary schools and we were foreigners. I came home crying to my parents, begging them to home school me as I was extremely intimidated. My father said, "I am sorry son, but I have to keep you going there or you will not develop social skills. You will thank me for this later in life." I could not and did not want to understand it at the time, but now I can see he turned out to be correct. I developed many friends in the Kenora community because of my time in the new school system.

I did not know how important the friends I made in this new community would become as grew up in a very abusive and toxic household. The friends I made became like family while their parents taught me what family was supposed to be. My father has an addictive personality, with his prime addictions being making money at business, drinking alcohol, and eating disorders. My father spent a lot of time at his first, primary business known as the main lodge. The first summer he was in business he had only one hundred customers all season. Our season was May to September which is the local fishing and hunting seasons. He decided he wanted to be the biggest and best operator in the area, which he worked at endlessly; he succeeded at this mission. Choosing success comes with a costly price of diminished relationships with family, locals, and suppliers. Within ten years he grew to having over two thousand customers in a season and gained a five-star rating. The government had inspectors that toured resort properties to rate them, based on quality of accommodations, boats/motors, food, and amenity/services.

Over time, my father bought an abandoned resort known as the island lodge. This resort was thirty-two miles from his base resort. The owners did not run it as a business, but they had kept renewing the business license for over twenty years. Our government is very protective of keeping the land as "Crown land," so we maintain our pristine fresh-quality air and space. A person must buy existing properties from another owner as the government will not release any more of its land. My father spent a lot of his time growing, renovating, and expanding this business to accommodate another two thousand guests each summer.

My father's third acquisition was a property next door to the main lodge known as the boutique lodge. This was a small boutique property that held less than sixty people. The owner had met his wife while playing in a travelling band that she had hired. They'd had a quick romance that had led to him marrying her quite suddenly before she passed away from sickness. This musician had no business experience and was put into a position that forced him to sell, as the resort eventually went into bankruptcy.

While my father was growing his businesses, my mother was helping him in operational duties. She worked in the Main Lodge overseeing the restaurant operations as well as housekeeping in the cabins and the main office. As the businesses grew, so did the pressure on my parents and their intimate relationship became toxic. My mother is also an alcoholic. My father would come home after heavy drinking and get quite verbally abusive with her. I used to cry watching the torment bestowed on my

Chapter Two: The upbringing

mother. As she got agitated, she took her anger out on me the next day. In my incredibly young years of five to ten, my mother would pin me down, calling me swear words, such as "you little S.O.B," while spitting on my face. When I turned eleven, I finally gained enough strength that she could not pin me down anymore, as I rolled out and flipped her over. I felt a sense of personal empowerment and said, "This abuse ends now as you can't hurt me anymore." The personal victory lasted a short amount of time as she decided to emotionally abuse me without the ability for physical harm anymore. She would wreck things that I valued, such as a favourite video game, snow mobile, and she burnt my first sport tickets in the fireplace. I especially recall wooden spoons getting broken over my forearms because I wanted a snack before dinner, after coming home from the school bus. I had an hour bus ride after getting out of school at 3:30 which allowed me to get quite hungry.

As the love between my parents faded, they found intimacies in other places. My father eventually found it with the female employees while my mother regularly found it with male employees and guests. I would hear fishing guides saying things in the morning such as, "Was it your turn to get a piece of the owner's wife yet?" The first time she left our family was with a freelance drummer from Winnipeg. I had no idea she was having an affair with this man until my father came into my room crying at 3 a.m. He said, "Your mother left me for another man and packed up all her bags." Apparently, this man was called to play drums with a band at the lodge, then stayed the rest of the summer at the local provincial park. I consoled my father until 6 a.m. and finally said, "I am sorry Dad, I have to get up and shower so I can get on my bus to school now." He cried to my sister and me every day all winter. Once summer began, he cried to the guests as they started to arrive in May. One guest finally pulled him a side and said, "You need to stop this sobbing as people come here to relax and get away from their own daily stresses ... You are dumping your marital issues on them." He also told my father that many were saying they could not wait to leave. He was a genuinely nice and sincere man, so I believe he was saying this out of care and love, not personal agitations. The man my mother left with lead to them having several affairs. My mother would leave with him, then break up and ask my father to come home … This happened at least three times over several years … But this time ended up being the biggest life-changing event.

It was life changing because she became pregnant with this man's soon-to-be daughter. Once she delivered the baby, he bailed as he was not interested in being a father to a baby. My mother called my father, crying, and asked to come home. She also wanted to bring this baby. My father said he would take her back but not with the baby she'd had with the man she left him for. She decided to give my baby sister up for adoption in Thunder Bay, Ontario.

To this day I have never met my sister. My father also insisted that my mother give him a third child to make up for her betrayal and for embarrassing him. Each time my mother came back home after an affair there was a familiar pattern. Things would be happy for the first three to four months while she tried to make peace. After a few months they would start fighting and eventually she would move into the spare room. This room used to be the master bedroom, so it had its own washroom. Then the abuse, alcohol—and same patterns would resume. The only bond I had with my mother was the harsh demands my father made on both of us. It was quite common for all of us to eat our meals in separate rooms instead of at the family dinner table. My father had a large four-bedroom house on an island so there was a lot of space for all of us to vacate ourselves to.

After a few months of being home my mother announced she was pregnant with my soon-to-be baby brother. I was already twelve, so by the time he was born there was a thirteen-year difference between him and me—which means an eleven-year gap with my sister. It is easy to see that the huge gap in our age also lead to a separation gap in our personal relationships. To this day I feel bad that he was not bred out of love but instead as a deal to amend past mishaps.

CHAPTER THREE:
And the high school years begin.

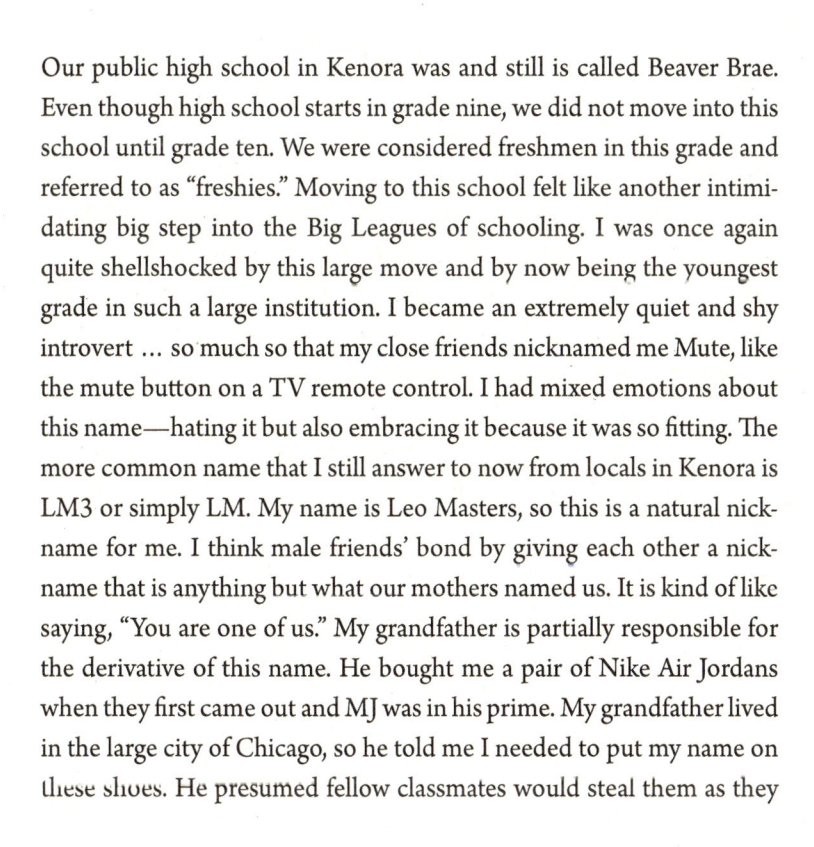

Our public high school in Kenora was and still is called Beaver Brae. Even though high school starts in grade nine, we did not move into this school until grade ten. We were considered freshmen in this grade and referred to as "freshies." Moving to this school felt like another intimidating big step into the Big Leagues of schooling. I was once again quite shellshocked by this large move and by now being the youngest grade in such a large institution. I became an extremely quiet and shy introvert … so much so that my close friends nicknamed me Mute, like the mute button on a TV remote control. I had mixed emotions about this name—hating it but also embracing it because it was so fitting. The more common name that I still answer to now from locals in Kenora is LM3 or simply LM. My name is Leo Masters, so this is a natural nickname for me. I think male friends' bond by giving each other a nickname that is anything but what our mothers named us. It is kind of like saying, "You are one of us." My grandfather is partially responsible for the derivative of this name. He bought me a pair of Nike Air Jordans when they first came out and MJ was in his prime. My grandfather lived in the large city of Chicago, so he told me I needed to put my name on these shoes. He presumed fellow classmates would steal them as they were hot commodities. I used black marker to put LM3on the back of them. Boys would yell "Hey look, there go the LM3's." Eventually the shoes wore out, but the nickname did not. I embraced it so much that I had personalized license plates with "ELMII" made.

Some of my best memories are from growing up in that school. The way I met one of my best friends, who is referred to as Bizzy, is quite funny. His father was fixing a television service at my parents' house, so he came down for a ride. My parents had an old-school round wooden hot tub in an enclosed porch room. This tub's heat was only turned on when being used and it was covered with a blue plastic bubble wrap to preserve its heat when not being used. Bizzy and I decided it would be a comical idea to toss my sister into this tub as a hazing and bonding of a new friendship. We thought this was hilarious, but my sister did not share our humour as the tub was apparently quite cold. Somehow, I knew this rascal and I were going to be great friends.

He was called Bizzy because he was quite busy with shenanigans and all the girls always wanted to get busy with this guy. I think there is an ultra-laser-beam chick magnet on him. There could be one hundred guys in a room, with all kinds of money and fame, and only one female—and she will dart right to him. It used to kind of piss me off, always being the invisible man when he was around, but I enjoyed his stories. I would also say that every bad thing I have ever done in my life, I did the first time with him. So yes, he is a great positive influence! And I dare not say what all the bad things were, as that is best left to the imagination. As we are all put on earth to keep growing and learning … I learn from all the crazy mistakes which also make funny stories.

The first vehicle I owned was a white GMC Jimmy. It was rebuilt and on sale at the local Kenora Chevy sales yard. I saved up for a few summers so had the money to buy it. I bought it and my father paid for the insurance for me. I later regretted the insurance, as he hid my vehicle when I came home with a haircut he did not approve of. I think the sides were cut noticeably short and it was unfamiliar and unacceptable to him. This Jimmy was hidden until my hair grew back in. I felt

Chapter Three: And the high school years begin.

this was unfair as I paid for the vehicle, but he said I could give him the insurance money back or wait until my hair grew—so I waited. That was one long week! My father purchased all his company vehicles from this dealership until they had a falling out. Once this happened, my father told me to sell my Jimmy so we could get a new car. We leased a black Mustang GT with tinted windows. It was an awesome hot-rod car. I thought this would elevate my "mute status" to "chick magnet," but it just made me EB3 (the mute) with a hot car! I was still so shy, I never had one girlfriend in high school.

My first rock concert was to our favourite heavy metal band, Metallica ... the best heavy metal band of all time. When I got to school one morning my friends said they had bought five tickets, and me being the sixth man made me the odd man out. They said, "Sorry buddy, you were still on the bus from Sioux Narrows, and we forgot about you." I used the payphone to call Ticketmaster and bought another ticket. It was in the very top nosebleed rafter by me. I said, "I do not care. We will all go up together and I still get to see my favourite band."

I was sitting in my seat during the warmups and a fellow came up to me and asked if I was alone. I very sceptically said yes, as Winnipeg can be quite the dangerous city. He asked if I would like to switch seats with him and he was in the "mosh pit" up front. I asked why and he said he wanted to be as far away from his brother as possible. We switched and I now had the best tickets with all the headbangers moshing around all concert long. The lead singer, James Hetfield, threw his guitar pick out and I caught it. One of my friends jumped a gate, so we watched the rest of the concert together. What a great stroke of luck! A fellow asked me to trade the pick for a plastic beer cup he claims one of the band members drank out of ... Yeah right buddy!!! Unfortunately, the pick and ticket were both things my mother later burnt for her unique punishment, but the memory will last forever.

I have a group of friends and we call ourselves the Mex Boys because we all got to go to a timeshare in Cancun on Spring Break. This trip was a bonding trip that still unites us to this day. None of us had ever seen hot beaches, hot girls, wet t-shirt contests, and party scenes like that. All I remember is Mexican bartenders yelling, "Poppers, poppers. It's tequila poppers …" Everywhere we went there was another popper. I was still shy even with these poppers. My friends would pick up girls and I would walk the beach home alone. Each hotel had security to protect their beachfront. After a while these guys got to know me and would let me walk through. They knew me as "The Canada Boy eh!" Police and security walk around with machine guns so they can pretty much call me anything they like! My grandfather gave me some sun oil to use that deepens your tan. I didn't realize how much closer to the sun Mexico was, so on the second day I put it on. I think people could feel the heat off me when I walked by with the sunburn. Maybe that is part of the reason I walked home alone each night lol. The ocean breeze was really refreshing so it worked out well.

The last and fondest memory I have in the end of high school was at a birthday party in Sioux Narrows. There was a girl in high school that was ridiculously hot. She was beautiful, smart, captain of the swim team, and really seemed to have it all. I jetted up to the beach in a small sixteen-foot Lund skiff while planning to be cool, trimming the motor up before sliding on the beach. I did not realize there was a rock in the bay until I hit it. All the birthday girl's friends were watching from her deck. Well, with all my infinite ways of trying to be cool I sure looked like a fool. I pulled the boat up on shore and had to call my father's lodge for help to tow it back. The crew that came drove me back, so I could pick up my Mustang to get home later. And wouldn't you know it, Miss Hottie came for a ride to keep me company and ease my broken ego. We had a great heart-to-heart in my car, and she kissed me when we pulled back up to the party. This was my first time kissing a girl and they say you never forget your first. I was on cloud nine with the angel until her friends came to the car and pulled her out. It was short but sweet.

Once I obtained my driver's license at sixteen, I felt a sense of freedom. It was quite common for me to leave to school Friday morning from Sioux Narrows and not return until Monday after noon.

Chapter Three: And the high school years begin.

There always seemed to be a friend's parent willing to let me spend the weekend ... Sometimes when the parents were away, they did not even know it. My friend, who was commonly nick named Nay-Day, and I made it a priority to find out when peoples' parents were away so we could orchestrate Friday and Saturday night bashes ... It really is amazing how many parents like to go away when they have no idea what they will be coming home to. I had one friend with the same last name that let me stay at his place quite often ... I think his parents almost embraced me as the weekend adopted son. The parents of my high-school best friend, Dicky Bird, used to let me stay quite a bit as well. Dicky Bird and Nay-Day were both good friends to have as they were accomplished athletes, which seemed to help me be accepted by the other athletes. I was far too lanky and awkward to play any sports myself.

And so ended the high school years. At least after the final high school Senior Prom. We all rented tuxedos and a stretched limo. My friend nick named Kipper had a weak stomach and puked on his pants, leaving the warm up we had before the prom at his mother's house. These pants were ruined so he had to put on a black pair of khaki pants ... He thought they matched, but the rest of us and everyone else at the dance assured him they did not. I guess he took one for the team as our dates refused to get into the car until he changed. I think I may have got my second ever kiss from my date that night ... so my night was much better than his! I was later told that most of the girls in high school had crushes on me, so I guess the shyness played in my favour ... One girl told me she thought it was funny that I had no clue.

CHAPTER FOUR:
The college years

I decided to enroll in the Confederation College Hospitality Management program in Thunder Bay, Ontario. This was a good course to teach me the fundamentals I would need to later take over the operations at my family's fishing resorts. Thunder Bay is approximately 550 kilometres from my hometown of Sioux Narrows so I could make the travel in one day of driving. I rented a three-bedroom apartment with three of my best friends from high school, the Mex Boys. I quickly learned that, of the bunch, I was the most dedicated to achieving my educational goals. We all knew how to party, and this city's bars had drink specials each night of the week. It did not take long for us to learn all the local watering holes and their best nights. We would start with cocktail hour in our apartment before hitting the streets. We started the week on "Fresh Meat Mondays," as that is when the new dancers would arrive for their scheduled week at The Gentleman's Strip Club. I had never experienced anything like this place, as it was full of men and women ready to party. Dancers sold tickets with numbers that the DJ would call out for personal dances. It seemed quite common for the dancers to be single mothers ... Therefore, I felt it was my obligated duty to purchase as many tickets as I could afford. I mean, baby needs some new shoes—right?! Thunder Bay seemed to have large Italian and Chinese populations. There were rumours of both these cultures

Chapter Four: The college years

sticking together in packs which we found to be true. We were often made to feel uncomfortable not being a part of "the pack." This left us to mostly stick to ourselves—forming our own "Wolf Pack," as referred to in the *Hangover* movie. I went through high school without smoking but now all my roommates smoked so I felt left out. I decided it would be cool to have one or two just before we went out. After two months, one of my roommates said it was my turn to purchase a pack because I keep mooching butts from them. This hit me like an alarm bell that it was time to quit this unhealthy habit. I went to the store and bought a carton, distributed it to each roommate to make us square, then never touched another butt in my life. I have always been a health addict that eats organically and exercises regularly, so I kept with my regimen. Girls from high school that used to call me the Mute took notice of my larger proportions from the gym, which gained me more positive attention. During Christmas break, I thought that maybe I had outgrown the "Muteness," but the name still stuck, as I could be quite shy at times.

All in all, this was a great year of bonding with my mates and learning in school. I say I was the most dedicated to my course, as I was on the Dean's List both semesters while my roommates were glued to the party zone. Two roommates dropped out of their courses while one changed his major.

This year was defined by one major moment. My mother called me in September to announce she was leaving my father for the final time. I told her I really hoped this was not another affair as it would be too detrimental to my young brother to endure what we had all had to go through. She promised it was not another man—she realized that she and my father were just not meant for each other. I promised if I found out it was another affair, I would never be able to speak to her again. Most people assumed this was because of the abuse I endured as a child, but it was merely to stop the toxic culture my parents embraced. When I came home for Thanksgiving, I found out she had packed her things to leave with another man she was already living with. She had lied to me—packing her bags when speaking with me on the phone in

September. I explained I could never speak to her again because I knew my father was too weak and would take her back when this relationship did not work out. To this day, I still have a distant and estranged relationship with my mother. I later came to realize that this burden hurt me in my intimate relationships with females all through my twenties. Most people considered me the ultimate, eternal playboy with multiple relationships, who lived a swinging lifestyle. My reputation made this true, but I have later come to realize that I had "mommy" baggage, causing me serious trust issues in relationships. It was easier for me to cut them off before anyone got hurt. I guess I tried to avoid my childhood past from recurring in my adult life.

During summer break my father hired me to be the restaurant/Main Lodge manager. I did not realize this until I returned home with my truck full of clothes and furniture. He told me all the servers were waiting for me to have my initial meeting with them. I was then rushed up to their dorm rooms for him to announce, "The boss has finally arrived." I was completely flustered and did not know what to say or do. He informed me that everyone had been panicked about how to set things up but that he had assured them I would soon be here to take control. I had worked in the main lodge kitchen before, but I had no idea how to manage, schedule, or instruct others in any of these managerial tasks. It is easy to see I was thrown to the wolves, so the summer was a disaster. I felt quite ashamed of how the restaurant was handled. Unfortunately, I did not even know what I did not know. I had no idea as to why it was so bad. Employees sensed the lack of confidence and took over the department. I can say I learned what not to do in my future responsibilities.

My second year of college started with mostly new roommates. One mate from the previous year returned to continue his diploma, which he finished. A second roommate from the previous year also returned to a new course, which he quickly dropped before the first holiday. We rented a two story, six-bedroom house from an Asian man, located near our college. This house was a continuous game of musical roommates

Chapter Four: The college years

as I think I had a total of ten throughout the year. It was an interesting time to keep track of expenses and cleaning duties. I once again maintained my status on the Dean's List through the chaos and college parties. The revolving door taught me how to be flexible to changes in lived circumstances. At the end of the day, plans and circumstances in our lives continue to change with little or no notice. It's not what happens to us in life but how we handle it that defines our character. Deep thoughts from a college boy eh?!

One memory that comes to mind is the night we rolled my Mustang GT. We were playing pool at a local Italian hotspot that had just been renovated. A "cougar" must have been impressed with my cue-pool talents and took an immediate shining to me. Apparently, her friends were not as impressed and decided to ditch her ... We were more than happy to offer her a ride home at closing time. The DJ announced you don't have to go home but you can't stay here, much like the lyrics of a popular song of the nineties. The backseat of my car was our only option, so she snuggled right into me as my friend drove. It was a stormy, rainy night as he drove down the highway. Another car cut in front of us, so my friend hit the brakes and we rolled into the ditch. Man did I ever learn how tough those Mustangs are built, as the roof caved in but no one was hurt. I called my father in a panic, and he said we were probably all in shock and should leave the car for the cops to find and recover it in the morning. When we got back to this girl's house she started crying and felt it was all her fault as she never should have been with us. Man, I sure know how to make women cry and blow a deal. Being the gentleman I am, I assured her it was okay ... even though I was the one that should be crying, now short of my hot rod! The car was rebuilt, and we were all lucky to walk away without a scratch. I never heard from her or my friend again after that night.

I was incredibly happy and proud to graduate on the Dean's List. I had mixed emotions as I knew the next steps would be challenging, heading into my career. I thought the most fun days of celebrating with my friends were behind me and my life would take a turn to adulthood.

We had one final trip funded by the college—a trip to Cancun in May. We worked in the local all-inclusive hotels to learn to adapt our education to the workforce. This was the most fun apprenticeship anyone could imagine! I had no idea what I was doing in any position, but customers would instantly come to me assuming I could help them. I guess I looked more familiar to what they were used to in their homelands of USA and Europe. Whilst our college was finishing after this trip, the American universities were on a reading break for final exams. This trip turned out to be better than spring break as it was less commercialized.

CHAPTER FIVE:
My illustrious life as a career man begins.

I am now fresh out of college with my Hotel and Hospitality Management diploma freshly in my hands. I had a ripe feeling that I was ready to take on the world. My grandfather flew from Chicago to Thunder Bay to watch my graduation ceremony. He was the only one in my family that could make it, but it meant so much that he made such a long journey. He said he was not surprised I had graduated on the Dean's List; with the amount of academic determination, I had always had. I cried tears of joy while we hugged before and after the ceremony.

I came home from Thunder Bay to find out I would be the assistant general manager of all operations at the main lodge main headquarters. I was not given a job description and did not know what this responsibility entailed. My father told me he was proud I graduated with such high honours—but to flush all of that down the toilet as my true education starts now. I kind of felt like all my hard work to obtain my diploma was rather meaningless so I asked what that meant. He said he was the mastermind of fishing resorts and had built the biggest and best in Canada. Then he went on to say that school professors can't understand real-life application … so throw the books out. "You need to be like your father, act like your father, and talk like your father." This later became the staple of our relationship as father and son, as well as boss to employee. I was purposely not given a description because I needed to be opened to mimicking his ways without preconceived notions.

I was also quite young and determined with my education, so I still attempted to apply all my education to the operations. I started a romance with my best friend from college and she was now the dining room manager. I felt knowledgeable in this department from my past summer. Let us call her by her nickname of Jewels. She was a highly intelligent woman, so we applied inventory control systems that the lodge had never seen. We soon came to realize there was a lot of theft and neglect, costing the business huge amounts of money. My father felt this was all meaningless and I should be spending more time with him instead of her. I soon came to realize that my training came from negative re-enforcement. I was not told what the expectations of my position were until I was told I was doing it wrong. I was never on time, was not on the docks with guides first thing in the morning ... did not greet guests in the morning, afternoon, and evening enough. I was also told the landscaping of the property, maintenance issues, and cabin cleanliness were all in disarray. At first, I thought it was just me feeling this way but then I noticed all the departments seemed to be in a hectic whirlwind of chaos. I felt a responsibility to make this environment better.

I hired a business consultant to come in and analyze both our main lodge and island lodge properties. She started by asking what my job was. I told her my position and she said, "Yes, but where is your list of daily duties?". I felt ashamed to not really know. She explained this was not my fault and that this was the first problem of the business. The person that is second-in-command is young, frantic, ill-prepared, and in over his head. Hearing this was bittersweet—the putdown felt bitter but hearing it was not my fault felt quite a bit sweeter. We noticed a common trend in each department. The main lodge was broken down into several departments: Main Office, Groundskeeping, Maintenance, Docks, Cabin Housekeeping, and Dining Room. The business later

Chapter Five: My illustrious life as a career man begins.

acquired a guest-service department to check in guests as well as airport transportation. Guests that decided to fly instead of driving either flew into the Winnipeg International Airport or International Falls Minnesota Airport. Her professional assessment was that the entire operation needed educated specialists to teach, train, and mentor each department's supervisor. She felt we needed job descriptions and manuals that could be transferred to each season. My father did not like or agree to any of this, so he sent us to the island lodge. He wanted us to assess this operation, but it felt more like he wanted us away from him at his main headquarters ... out of his hair, so to speak.

We soon came to realize that everyone at the island lodge seemed very unhappy and agitated. Her observations concluded that the resort manager lead with a dictator-type of style, instilling fear. We also came to realize he had been stealing money and assets from the property. Apparently, he was so far away from the main lodge that he was not supervised. At the time, I did not realize all these observations would lead to my transfer to this position the next summer.

The season ended with both lodges closing in October. We were now to learn the closing procedures as well as getting ready for winter fishing and hunting sport shows. I felt quite burnt out from a long summer and needed a break. In the summer months we work seven days per week and sporadic hours, as there is always something that needs to be attended to. During these long days I was told that we need to make hay while the sun shines in the summer, then we get to take extended breaks when things shut down in the fall. I was shockingly disappointed that this seemed to no longer be the case. I decided that I should at least be able to work five days instead of seven to have some rest ... I took it upon myself to make this happen despite the grief I would take for it. After all, we are all human, and all humans need time to give our systems a break.

CHAPTER SIX:
Winter months begin.

Our winter schedule felt remarkably like a rock band's tour schedule of long-haul travelling. We left the lodge in a van after New Year's Day and did not return home until after Easter at the end of March. Our van was loaded with sport show displays, personal luggage, and marketing brochures. We attended thirteen to eighteen shows in cities across the Midwest USA. The average show could be Monday to Wednesday followed by another show from Thursday to Sunday. We worked three to four days and broke down our display on the last day to drive to the next city. We would wake up, set up the display in the new convention center, and start selling that afternoon.

The schedule was quite busy and offered little personal time. Despite this, I enjoyed the travelling and exploring new cities very much. We got to stay in three-to-four-star hotels while enjoying nice dinners in restaurants each night. While we worked extremely hard it was nice to have restaurant service, daily housekeeping, and sometimes help with laundry. I have always been extremely healthy and found time to hit fitness centres in the hotels or close by. My girlfriend was surprised that I would come home in better shape than when I left. My father and both employees I travelled with were surprised at how remarkably well I did with the sales. They all expected I would be out partying and did not anticipate me taking on the challenges so seriously. The manager of the island lodge was a Lebanese

Chapter Six: Winter months begin.

man who was quite the salesman. He would call people out of the aisles to come and see him with quite a candid and humorous style.

I kept up with him, toe-to-toe for new sales each week—which I think eventually agitated him. He was an extremely competitive man and was used to getting most of the new sales. His competitiveness led to sarcastic and belittling remarks as an attempt to bring me down. This somehow sparked me to strive to be even harder … I learned a lot from both him and my father and put the newly found tools to work. I am a Leo, and it is my nature to fight hard, with an internal competitiveness, when pushed against a wall. I can say I appreciated his reverse psychology as it helped me to be much better in sales and PR all throughout my career. This salesman used to chirp, "Don't worry about the sales, eh boy. Your daddy will give you it all anyways."

It was quite common for us to go to dinners with guests and suppliers in each city we were at. It did not surprise me that the suppliers wanted to entertain us to build a bond with their customer. It did, however, surprise me that guests would take us to expensive restaurants and insist on paying the bill. They felt that we showed them such a good time in the summer that they wanted to show us gratitude. I now started to understand what my father meant about working hard in the summer to reap the rewards in the winter. We worked extremely hard but also had a good lifestyle to show for it.

At the end of the first winter, my father told me that the island lodge manager would not be returning because of the past summer's theft. He also told me I would be taking his position so I should be prepared to pack my bags to live on the island this summer. This was quite surprising because all the previous summer and winter my father had kept defending what a great promoter and asset to the company this man was. I somehow felt I was arguing with my father on behalf of all of us that knew better. I think this man saw the writing on the wall—that he was going to be replaced—with how well I was doing and me being a part of the family. So, I am not sure if he quit or got fired but I don't think it really mattered.

CHAPTER SEVEN:
My career as a resort general manager begins.

Our summer season opens at the walleye/pickerel fishing opener which is also around Canada's May long weekend. This was on average the third Saturday of May, which is also the week prior to America's long Memorial Day weekend. We took our opening staff out as soon as the ice melted enough for us to drive by boat. The winter months get quite cold and up to forty-below temperatures, so we get enough ice to drive a vehicle on. The ice and snow melt in the spring, allowing us to launch boat/motors so we can drive on the lake. I had myself, the head cook, lead maintenance man, his assistant, groceries, and tools so we could start up the main lodge. This lodge is on an island with no hydroelectricity, so we had to start up the 200kw diesel generator. We also had to start up the water lines which could still be frozen in some parts from the frozen ground. On a good year we could have the main lodge and cabins opened in less than a week.

Once the lodge's utilities were operational, we would bring in the rest of the opening crew. Dockhands, servers, bartenders, cooks, dishwasher, housekeeping all came in to clean the resort. Cabins and rooms had to be cleaned thoroughly and set up for the first guests. The main lodge also had to be cleaned and set up for bar and meal services. The

Chapter Seven: My career as a resort general manager begins.

dockhands did groundskeeping duties which required lawn mowing, cutting wood, changing garbage cans, and cleaning the fish-filleting house. Once the grounds were cleaned it was time to start launching the boats. Each seventeen-foot Outfitter had a 40 or 50hp engine with VHF radios, live wells, fish graphs, and antennas. Each boat also had to be equipped with boaters' safety equipment. Guests that did not have a guide came back to the lodge for shore lunch each day. We had a full-time shore-lunch cook by the boathouse area.

For those not familiar with the "shore lunch," it is exactly what it sounds like. Fishing guides pull onto the shoreline of an island. The guides filet all the fish that were freshly caught, then start an open fire. This becomes a makeshift kitchen where guides drop the fish into hot oil over the fire along with a potato and cut fresh vegetable recipe and beans. There are also freshly made cookies for dessert. Northern resorts have become quite famous for the shore-lunch experience and many guests say this is a primary reason for returning. I can assure you that no one has a better recipe than our family's resorts as it has been passed down through so many generations of guides.

I was quite intimidated by the idea of starting the season. Many of the staff returned from the previous seasons so they knew the resort quite well. I barely knew where the washer and dryer were, so I was orientated by others. Most of the employees were quite a bit older than me, as I was only twenty. I was very shaky and awkward giving my opening speeches and I could tell they sensed my shyness. In usual circumstances, management trains employees from their experience and this establishes the hierarchy relationship. In this case it was backwards, so the employees ran over me quite a bit this summer. I repeatedly called back to the main lodge for help and direction and was told the only way to learn is by trial and fire. I really felt like I was fed to the wolves or thrown in the water with no life vest. This was an extremely challenging year, but it later made me quite a bit stronger. I really had to learn the operation from the ground up, so I understood every aspect of it.

LION OF THE LAKE

My girlfriend from college came to help me at the resort. We made a deal that I would handle all the outside operations—guides, docks, grounds, boat runs, and guest services. She would handle all the inside operations—the dining room, bar, food orders, and housekeeping. We lasted almost four years, with the first being at the main lodge and about three summers at this resort. I know many relationships that end in business, and this would be one of them. She demanded that I stay away from all inside operations while she was outlandish in the outside operations. It felt like we were butting heads in every direction. I had the main responsibility of the resort, and she was quite headstrong. She proclaimed I would not be attending any more sport shows because I had to be at home with our future children. She also made it clear I would not be naming my first son after me because of all the trauma I faced being named after my father. This felt quite aggressive to someone that I had not even proposed to, so I told her in the spring before I headed back to the island lodge that I would be going alone. She cried and said she knew it was coming. I was surprised at how well her parents handled it when they came to pick her up. They said they would always love me. She stayed friends with me and helped me construct my resume the first time I left on my own. I believe she has gone on to achieve many great things and started her own recruiting business. After we broke up, I saw it to be my destiny to sew my wild oats and kind of felt like I had just awoken and broke out of a shell.

CHAPTER EIGHT:
Freshly groomed and ready to take it all on

I spent almost ten years managing island lodge operation in the summers and doing the winter sport show seasons in the winter. I can now share some of the many great adventures I endured during the on- and off-season times.

Each spring and fall I moved all my personal belongings from the island lodge for the summer to various winterized cabins at the main lodge for the winter … I was quite the travelling gypsy, moving at least once to twice a year for the rest of my life. People could not believe we lived on an island all summer, but it became quite familiar. We had approximately twenty employees, fifty to one hundred guests, as well as the local customers coming off the lake for meals and refreshments. After being on the island, it felt quite uncommon to hop into a vehicle and drive through streets … We not only work together out there but we become a team, with a family-like culture. I used to tell the employees we are a chain, and a chain is only as strong as its weakest link. I used to hire, train, mentor, discipline the employees, and ultimately had the responsibility of terminating some. It was quite amazing when I had to let someone go as it really seemed like the whole island had voted them out, like a *Survivor*-type reality show. If one person was not pulling their weight, they also got shunned in their personal life after work hours. It seemed almost like a celebration to the employees that the bad seed was removed so we could resume our positive environment.

Over the years, I assembled a team that became quite loyal to me and the resort. This is unusual in a seasonal business as most employees sign a contract for the summer and move onto other ventures in the winter. The ones that left for good seemed to refer friends and family to replace themselves. I do not know if they all quite understood how much grief I had to endure to give them fair compensation. I was always told that anything above minimum wage was a luxury and anyone wanting more was scamming me. I came to realize some people are worth more given their experience, efforts, and responsibilities. I had to create new titles to justify why someone was worth more compensation. Perhaps the employees did recognize it and this is why they became so loyal … I fought for them, so they felt compelled to work hard for me.

I was referred to as the "GQ Manager," after the men's fashion magazine. I used to watch James Bond movies which, to date, is still my favourite series. My father's best friend owned the largest and most well-operated marina in the area. I believe he became the largest Mercury and Lund dealer in our area as well as across Canada. I observed that he was always well dressed in a button-up dress shirt, slacks, and nice shoes. I emulated his style as well as James Bond. My hair and nails were always well groomed, shirts and pants pressed, and shoes shined. Guests used to laugh to the guides that they would try to outdress me when they got back to work in the city. I order my martinis dirty with both vodka and gin, two olives, and neat but bruised. I will be happy to teach any novice what this means for presentation. I followed my grandfathers' advice that a man's shoes and nails should be buffed and shined, as those are the foremost first impressions. I also used whitening toothpaste and put highlights in my hair with a spikey kind of style. As you can tell, I stood out like a sore thumb amongst fishermen in their overalls and sun caps. This style seemed to get me much respect from my peers, guests, and colleagues. Perhaps ZZ Top is right that "Women Go Crazy Over a Sharp Dressed Man," as I enjoyed that attention as well!

Chapter Eight: Freshly groomed and ready to take it all on

As I stated earlier, the island lodge t was an abandoned lodge that my father purchased with the goal of renovating. In the early years, the cabins were old logs with three individual hotel-type rooms and a common screened-in porch. These cabins were incredibly old and infested with mice, no air conditioning, and got quite hot. Each winter we tore down cabins and rebuilt brand new ones that were very modern. Today, each cabin has satellite televisions, air conditioning, full modern bathrooms, and front decks. There are also two outdoor hot tubs. The main lodge was also torn down and rebuilt with a large dining room, two bars, fireplace, store, kitchen, and employee rooms above for the servers. The main level has a wraparound outdoor deck. The bottom level has an exercise room for guests, which almost never gets used as they are out fishing. My manager's estate was built above with a bedroom, living room, bathroom, and personal exercise room. If all of this sounds awesome that is because it really is. We turned an abandoned, run-down camp into the hottest and most pristine entity in the area. This was built with hard work, very many loans, and patience! I took it as a challenge for the service standards to match the facilities. We had a young boy that used to run to catch the boats when they came into the docks. Both of his parents worked at the resort, employed as a guide and cook, and his brother was a maintenance person while his sister became a server. I kind of feel like our resort helped raise those three as the father was quite distant and the mother left after my first season. This boy was too young to work but left an impact that remains at the resort to this day. The dockhands would see him running to the boats and raced to beat him. Being greeted at the docks and hot servers became my claim to fame throughout my career. If only the guests knew I had nothing to do with the exquisite dock service, but it was a kid that made us shine! I suppose I can take credit for hiring pretty and talented servers. They worked split shifts for breakfast and dinner and suntanned on the docks while the fishermen where on the lake. I think the guests thought I staged the girls for their viewing when they returned off the lake or came in for lunch. This was also a mere coincidence. But if I had to be known as the GQ Playboy resort operator, then so be it!

CHAPTER NINE:
Tales of the North

Many may not believe some of the great many things I have done and experienced throughout my journey, but I will attempt to tell them to the best of my memory now.

I was in Fargo, North Dakota, at a sport show when our taxidermist came walking down the aisle with his hotshot son strutting alongside. Our taxidermist was second generation with the most well-known and respected business of its kind in Winnipeg, Manitoba. His son was going to university in Grand Forks, North Dakota, so he brought him to meet some of the lodge owners. This punk had spikey hair and a cocky grin but was well dressed in the company's logoed V-neck sweater and button-up shirt with Docker pants. I thought *this guy is full of himself* but was drawn into his confidence and somehow knew we could become friends. He later informed me that his dad had told him, "That will be your best friend someday so stick close to him." I thought his dad told him this merely because we sent them many fish mounts from our guests ... But his father had an insight that came true to this day. Talk about father's intuition eh!

At the sport shows there were many of us young guys in our early twenties attending. You would think there would be a rivalry from all of us competing for the same customers. But instead, there became a brotherhood that formed known as the SOS club. The taxidermist

Chapter Nine: Tales of the North

thought this would be a fitting name after the Son of Sam's serial killer ... But we were all Sons of Sam's, being at least second generation into the resort businesses. We all had different brands of resorts, with ours being full service, five stars, while others were strictly fly outs to remote lakes, one houseboat rental, and so forth. We helped each other at the shows when someone was looking for an experience, we did not offer by taking them to the appropriate SOS establishment. This became a win/win for us and the consumers looking for the appropriate fishing experience in their budget. We worked hard during the long show hours then became a band of misfits at night. I say, *you know you have a best friend when you can leave a brief case full of cash and your girl for a week and know neither one has been touched when you return.* I would have a hard time naming which one is the absolute best friend in the group as they all are. These are all hardworking men with great spirit and character. We act toward women like gentlemen and usually fight to pay each round of drinks when they come. There are just over a handful of us. Many others have come out with us but just did not fit in. Sometimes they were too cheap or derogatory to women and others around. We did not sacrifice sheep or have rookie initiations but there was an unsaid code of honour to get in ... There is still to this day one known as "The Rookie," as he was an original SOS's younger brother and did have to get sworn in. I was the only single one, so these were my wingmen—which was pretty much all it took for me! I know, I am tough to impress eh ... He also bought many rounds of drinks at the beginning so was sworn in. When I got married, this little son of a gun left an IOU to his parents in their cash register and flew to Las Vegas for my wedding ... He also later came for my divorce party in the same city only a couple of years later. I guess marriages are short lived when you get hitched at a Little Chapel of The West in Las Vegas! I can tell you the divorce trip was even better but cannot say why because what happens in Vegas stays in Vegas ...

When I married this woman, I was surprised that pretty much every single one of them came to my wedding. Oddly enough, every single one of them except for the Rookies brother who was apparently too busy pounding dents out of his houseboats. I planned to have my bachelor party in Vegas the weekend before Canadian Thanksgiving … We then planned to have our wedding at my family's resort on the Thanksgiving weekend. Because I was grossly mistreated by my father and brother, my girlfriend and I had to move to the Greater Toronto area. This left us emptyhanded for a wedding venue. I tossed out the idea that all my best friends were planning Las Vegas for my bachelor party so we should just get hitched there … I thought never in a million years would she agree, but low and behold she loved the idea. The night before our wedding, my friends rented a stretched Hummer and brought me to the best gentleman's club in Las Vegas. We had a VIP table and they had girl after girl lined up to dance for me. This beautiful woman from South America sat on my lap for over an hour. I thought my friends hired her to sit with me, but they later told me that she insisted on sitting with me and to keep the other girls away. This girl proposed to me and said I should not marry a Canadian girl because all North American women are just out for themselves. She also told me she would devote herself to me and give me anything I ever wanted without denying me any time. She looked like the Columbian wife on *The Modern Family* show, so my head was spinning. My future father-in-law and fiancé's mother's boyfriend were at the same table, so I thought this was set up as a test of faith. But she convinced me that she was sincere. Out of respect to my future wife and the family that was there, I immediately dismissed the idea. I also did not trust a woman that proposes to a man the night before he is getting married … especially a foreign woman I just met at a strip club. Nonetheless, the offer was quite flattering! Little did I know that my wife would not be so loyal to me later into our marriage. I think I still made the best ethical decision, especially with the beautiful son that she produced with me.

CHAPTER 10:
The many wild adventures

I have to say this is the most fun of my chapters to write. This is also the chapter where the people who experienced these adventures with me will enjoy the walks down memory lane as they read it. I have been brainstorming my adventures throughout my twenties, so these are in no order.

As my father used to entertain guests at his house, it appeared it was my time to follow in his footsteps at the island lodge. I was informed that a guest arriving was the sales manager for *The Bob and Tom Radio Show* aired out of Indianapolis, Indiana. I had never heard of this show, but he informed me they were a well-followed duo that were known for being quite comical with wise jokes. This gentleman also informed me that they were looking for venues to host giveaways for their show. Let's just call this man Kendall, as that seemed to be what everyone else called him. I felt awkward hosting this man and his son as I did not have a private dining area, so I cleared out a boardroom upstairs of the main lodge. My head cook that summer was from Newfoundland—to say the least, his appearance and cuisine were quite raw. I thought I totally bombed on this dinner, but Kendall seemed quite impressed with the effort.

This gentleman was so impressed that he eventually offered me two tickets to the Indy 500. My friend and I flew to Indianapolis and could not believe what we were about to experience. The first day was spent at a Miller Lite party with Playboy and the Miller models. The Playmate of The Month was signing autographs in the centerfold of this month's magazine. Security guards made sure we could not get close, but the Miller models were quite flirty, and the free beer fit right in my budget. We were then carted off to a field outside of the racetrack where the Third Eye Blind band was performing ... Apparently this was the field that the weekend RV fans set up camp to stay for the race. I quickly realized this was a real redneck sport, so I flipped my hat backwards and took my shirt off. I don't think anyone was too impressed as they seemed more entertained by the band. We finished the day by getting to see some of the cars getting prepared for the race; we both got to sit in the cars that were being fired up for future races ... or at least my friend did, as I was too tall to fit inside them.

The next day was Carb Day, where the race cares raced went around the track and were timed to determine their starting positions. Kendall did not think we would be too interested, so he took us to a concert his station was hosting. I did not realize we would have VIP passes ... These passes gave us backstage access to see the bands conducting interviews. We also got to see their tour busses and the girls in line for a potential tour after their performance. Coors Light hosted a wet t-shirt contest that was quite entertaining to say the least. Unfortunately, my breasts were not perky enough to enter so we were mere spectators. I seem to remember the band Fly Leaf opening, with Three Days Grace headlining. There was a VIP tent set up with complimentary beer in between sets. Our passes gained us access to this tent. A band we did not know was playing so my friend, Bizzy, and I stayed in the tent. I was sitting by myself on the corner of the bar when an Irishman with no pass approached me. I thought maybe he was lost but he was headed right to me. He asked where I was from and what I did, so I replied, "Canada and I run a fishing resort." He asked if I was a "faggot" or I fished. I could tell he was quite juiced as he asked several times, with more vigor each time. What saved me, you ask? I had to tell him that a Northern

Chapter 10: The many wild adventures

Pike did not have stripes, as that is a Musky, and that Northern have spots from mouth to tail. He smiled and said he came to pick up chicks or fight and there were no chicks, so he was attempting to start a fight. Who knew a fish from Canada could save me in Indianapolis! When I headed back to the concert field, a Coors Light model approached me, proclaiming herself to be lost. Well, how could I not help a beautiful girl in distress? I took her by the hand to where I was sitting and, as we could not hear each other, we headed back to the tent. Kendall and Bizzy were disappointed that I missed most of the headline until they saw me arm and arm with my newfound friend. Even the cauliflower-eared Irish man was impressed as he watched from a distance. A gentleman never kisses and tells, which is a good thing because she wouldn't even let me kiss her when I walked her back to her car. So, I went from hero in the tent to zero in the parking lot.

The race on the last day was kind of boring as we had headphones on to block the noise. The track was so long that cars came zooming by every few minutes, so I do not think we made it through the whole race. The band, Stained, opened the race which was quite the highlight. We went to a bar downtown hosted by a new energy drink company. Apparently, Mario Andretti's sons placed second and third and were there to celebrate with Ludacris and other celebrities in the back room. We never got to see the celebrities, but it was exciting knowing we were at the same venue. The salesman for the energy drink kept buying us drinks with his newest flavour and played wingman for us with his models. These girls were far more interesting than the celebrities, so we were quite content in the outsiders' area. We still had our VIP passes from the races, so perhaps they all thought we were more important than we were. It's not that I am a liar, but I know no one likes to be wrong so I allowed them to be right! On our way out, one of the models insisted on escorting us to our taxicab as she kissed me. Unfortunately, a manager stopped her from leaving the bar as she was expected to help clean up the energy drink station. She gave me her number and invited us on a yacht party the next day, but we had to leave.

LION OF THE LAKE

We became quite famous in Green Bay, Wisconsin, at a local bar close to our hotel and sport show venue. They used to play the Canadian national anthem when we came in and had chairs reserved for us at the bar. I also got to know the servers at the Green Bay Hooters, so they would come and sit in my booth in their outfits. I thought this would draw attention from the potential fishermen who would then talk to me ... but soon came to realize it drew everyone but customers. Each year, people would come and ask where my girls were—so the bright orange draws attention. We went to our local watering hole to watch the Superbowl after the weekend sport show was over. They hosted a Budweiser draw for the NHL All-Star game the next weekend to anyone purchasing a bucket of beers. The owner liked us so much he gave two of us the tickets. I invited one of my Hooter girls, but she shot me down because of her boyfriend's disapproval. Some guys can be so selfish, eh?! So, I brought one of my best friends, known as Terry Eyed—yes, the cross-eyed bandit when he drinks. No, seriously, he goes cross eyed!

I did not realize how much these NHL tickets would keep giving us all weekend. They included our flights and hotel as well as tickets in the Budweiser suite. We met the former St. Louis Blues captain who had previously stayed at a hotel in our hometown Kenora. I had no idea who he was but Terry Eyed recognized him from over fifteen years ago. It was super cool to sit with all the high rollers. A rep from Skyy Vodka asked if we were going to the Sheryl Crowe concert after the game. We had no idea there was a concert, so she gave us free tickets. Of course, I had to get her number to thank her properly and make sure we did not get lost ... It was an outside concert, and our rep blew us off to party with the owners of the Florida Panthers, as that is where the All-Star game was hosted. But do not fear, as she was from Chicago, and we stayed in touch ... She was quite the host when we came to the windy city for our All-Canada Sport Show events. She also came to visit me at the island lodge one summer. She was a former soccer goalie and helped my team celebrate after winning a weekend tournament.

Chapter 10: The many wild adventures

Unfortunately, she ditched me for one of my teammates, but such is life! I was giving my team a ride back into Kenora after we celebrated our championship when I saw her making out with him in the back of the boat. I escorted everyone to the local bar and when I came back, she was lying in the boat by herself, passed out. She was crying because she thought I ditched her and thought I was the one she was making out with in the boat. The soccer team she played for was Michigan State, so I guess they do not teach them how to hold their liquor in that state!

Apparently, everyone at all three resorts were doing such a terrible job that my father decided to hire a new general manager for the chain. I was unaware of this until a Dutch man came to the resort mid-morning, introducing himself and giving his title. He was quick to drill me on the status quo of all menu items' cost per serving, all menu price breakdowns, and my resort's mission statement. I had learned all of this in college but had been told by my father to flush all of this down the toilet as my only education was to come from him. I thought this man was a practical joke, as my father has a bizarre sense of humour. The more I did not take this man seriously, the more agitated he became. Once we started to understand each other he informed me he was sent out to put me in my place. He was told that I was a know-it-all spoiled brat who had become too cocky. After a few weeks he realized this was not the case and complimented me at how well I had the operations in hand. I did learn quite a bit from his composure and strong commanding structure. Unfortunately, it did not work so well with such small-town lifestyles and resorts that had never been used to this kind of structure. Within two years he left, but I tried to implement his style and structure in a softer way. He told me to always inform subordinates what to expect, then inspect that it was completed to satisfaction. Coming from a military family myself, I really came to respect his attention to detail. My father still believes I always hated him … but in truth, it was just a rough beginning that matured into a healthy working relationship. I think he concluded that it was the owner that needed the discipline to change, and this is why he left.

LION OF THE LAKE

    I have a friend that was drafted by an NHL team first round and played for Team Canada in the World Juniors tournaments. He was a couple of years older than me, so I did not get to know him until later in his career. Let's just call him Duke because he played for the English Super Ice Hockey League when I went to visit him, and the British seem to mimic the royal families. I started my vacation on a family trip in London with an employee of the main lodge. He found out he had terminal pancreatic cancer and wanted to see his British family one last time before passing. We got to see many of the Queen's castles and historic sites around the city. This fellow decided to give me a royal tour of his own. He took me to a bar down a quiet cobblestone alley that was really off the beaten path. Once inside, a host showed us to a private booth seating where I ordered a bottle of champagne. Two beautiful girls came and sat with us, so I guess it pays to be a high roller drinking the good stuff. The girl beside me took an immediate liking to me as we danced the night away. I do not think she took her eyes or hands off me the whole time. Once I paid the bill and was heading to leave, she also grabbed her purse to come with me. I know I am smooth and charming but figured my Canadian accent must have really paid off. Once I paid the bill it was the most expensive, I have seen, so apparently my friend decided I was treating both of us to a clip joint. I will let you leave the ending of that to your imagination, and you can imagine why she stayed glued to me. Because I was from out of town, she insisted on escorting me back to my hotel.

    Fresh off my family's vacation, with an empty wallet, it was time to go and see the illustrious hockey star. I took a train from London to Manchester. The train was delayed so I had to take a taxi to the hockey arena. With luggage in hand, I knocked on the doors, explaining I knew one of the players. He was injured so he came to meet me at a side entrance and laughed that I should not be there. Because he was injured, we sat in the players' seats. Apparently one of his teammates from Cleveland, Ohio, was homesick and leaving the team. The fans thought I was his replacement, so I ended up signing autographs. I did

Chapter 10: The many wild adventures

not know if it was worse to reject signing or mislead them, but he told me to play it up. I was officially an all-star athlete for one night. After the game we went to a bar where the team gets complimentary cocktails and food. There were so many girls around, my head was spinning. Duke told me to pick which group of girls I wanted, as they thought I was the fresh blood coming to the team. He then explained the pros and cons of each group of girls. From the clip joint the day before to the land of puck bunnies tonight—my hormones were really spinning. I ended up hanging out with a girl that looked like Madonna from her "Tell Me "Music video … Is England a great country or what? She brought me back to my friend's condo and came in to join the festivities. From there she taught me to play Truth or Dare. I did not think I could be truthful with a girl that hot, so I stuck to the dares. The lure of a beautiful woman can really dare you to do a lot of crazy things.

I had so much fun in Manchester that I went back the next season to his new team in Belfast, Ireland. This team was sponsored by Harp Lager so they had an iced garbage can of beer in the locker room after each game. I was allowed a team pass to join them. Not that I had any desire to watch naked jocks shower and change, but the free beer and stories were priceless. When we left the stadium, fans were waiting outside. One girl asked my friend to sign her chest and the coach told him "Just in an appropriate area." Other girls asked for a kiss on the cheek and so the coach said it was okay. After the kiss she wept and said, "I will never wash this cheek again." I could now see why these guys had such big egos as they were celebrities in this turf. My last night there we hopped a train to Dublin. It was the last train because we were in a pub all day at the train station and kept missing each departure There was a huge celebration in Dublin, so every bar was overly packed. I did not realize my British pounds currency was not accepted here so I had no money and bars were too busy to accept credit cards. After getting bumped out of every place I went, I ended up lying on the street where the duke found me. All the hotels were sold out and the train station was closed so we were officially homeless. Luckily, one night manager recognized Duke from the team, so we ended up in some large penthouse of a ritzy hotel. The cab driver bringing us around must have been IRA as he went on a rant about the British trying to run all the UK. This gave me a flashback of the black cab tour I took in Belfast. Anyone who ends up there needs to take this tour. Tanks and military helicopters are surrounding the areas. There is a huge battle between the English and Irish supporters in that city, so you do not want to end up on the wrong side of the street. These two trips really bonded the duke and me. So much so that I attended his wedding in Minneapolis, Minnesota, not far after he retired from hockey. He apologized for not having me in his wedding party as they had to split people with him and his wife. I really had no idea he thought that much of our friendship and was just honoured to be there. I think his wife's sister may still hate me for mistaking her for her mom … someone pointed in that direction, telling me to ask the wife's mom where to sit. The best man said, "Don't worry. I covered your back and told her you are known to say a lot of stupid things." If that is covering me, I would hate to see his idea of throwing me under the bus because that is mine.

Kendall from Indiana brought his family to the island lodge one summer. His nephew was from California and had a real city-slicker look that did not fit into a fishing resort environment. The Duke and I were playing pool and I think he slipped something in our drink. We both blacked out and woke up in my room feeling quite ill the next day. The family checked out before I got up in the morning, so I never saw him again.

I finished a sport show in Minneapolis and had a couple of days before the next show started in Green Bay. I decided to look for some new dude and scout the hotties at The Mall of America. As I was walking, an attractive middle-aged woman approached me asking if I had ever modelled before. I thought one of my friends was on a higher level, spotting me and playing a joke. She was genuinely a talent scout and told me I should come to the hotel she was at for a photoshoot to make a portfolio. I later saw her out that night and she urged me

Chapter 10: The many wild adventures

to come, claiming I had that tall height and features to make a career. Unfortunately, I was heading to Green Bay so did not go … I was also skeptical about standing out in front of other professional models. I was very flattered at the offer and kept her business card for quite some time just in case … I mean, adding the "Zoolander" title to my resort manager resume could have been cool.

I was staying at the Hyatt Regency in Milwaukee, Wisconsin. The vice president of the Miller Brewing company was a customer of ours and gave us front row seats to a Bucks game. A fellow employee with me had a beer dumped on him by a basketball and simply did not care. You really have not seen a live basketball game until you have seen it from seats like these. Anyone who knows me personally would know Brett Favre is my favorite athlete of all time. When I was getting onto the elevator, leaving my hotel to go to the game, I saw him getting into the elevator. He smiled, jumped in, and pushed the button to close the door. These were glass elevators so I could see him going down … He laughed and shook his head at me while wagging his finger back and forth to say that I missed out. Apparently, he was throwing out balls at the halftime of the soccer game next door. So, I kind of, sort of, almost met Brett Favre and shared an elevator with the Ironman of Football.

A gentleman that owns a cabin close to the main lodge enjoyed entertaining us at top-rated steak houses when we came to the Chicago O'Hare sports show. He seemed to know the owner, but the owner had a way of making everyone feel they knew him. This gentleman owner became so popular that he opened a chain of steak houses. I was in his newest restaurant at the Double Tree Resort, quite close to the airport and Rosemont Convention Centre where our show was taking place. After dinner I stayed in the martini bar to indulge in a night cap. A camp owner that I only ever saw in Chicago saw me sitting alone, so he joined me. About two tables over from us were two black African American women who were quite attractive. As my late grandmother was also African American, I thought I could use my Canadian accent to lure them. The fellow with me was much more interested than I was and insisted they were prostitutes, as that profession is known to come into these expensive steak houses. I got up to go to the restroom and could hear them talking about which men looked like their best prospects. When I came back, the fellow sitting with me was now at their table and seemed to be negotiating with them. I could tell he had no interest in me joining and especially not offering them anything for me, so I decided to depart for the evening. I later found out his wife is a former prostitute so I guess this is how he could spot them so easily.

I went to visit my aunt in Los Angeles when I was in my early twenties. She lived in West Hollywood and gave me quite the tour of LA and all it has to offer. I did not realize until later that West Hollywood has the largest population of homosexuals in California. Before I knew this, I just thought all the dudes were friendly and making me feel welcome as a visitor … I later realized they felt I was fresh meat! My aunt had me dressed in leather pants and a see-through mesh shirt at a clothing store on Melrose Place. The salesmen kept telling me how great I looked as he tried to sell me this attire. I did not realize she brought me there knowing the guy told her how attractive I was, and this was all a set up. She also brought me to a local sex shop that had all kinds of toys I never knew existed. One mannequin was in a human-size bird cage, tied up in leather and looking like The Gimp from the *Pulp Fiction* movie. She also brought me to a bar called the Viper Room that Johnny Depp owned. And a bar/concert hall that hosted many popular bands such as The Doors. It was like a Hollywood movie was coming to life as I saw it all firsthand. I could see how LA sets the trends in music, fashion, and culture. It was equally exciting and intimidating. Everyone felt they were the next movie star or had the next Hollywood script. It was quite pretentious.

CHAPTER 11:
The wild and fun times continue.

Somehow my birthdays around the family and business were a bit borderline, with huge ups or downs, so I never quite knew what to expect. On my twenty-third birthday my father asked me to jump in the boat to head into Kenora for a birthday surprise and lunch. Along the way he gave me a $200 cheque written to his name that he signed over to me, as we had the same name. He explained that a born-again Christian had stolen some articles from the main lodge a few years before and wanted to pay back my father to repent her sins. I was so upset that my father would give me a jaded cheque with absolutely no meaning or thought put into it from him. He is known to regift presents or have others purchase them on his behalf. He waited until we were halfway to Kenora to present this to me so I could not demand to go back home. The more upset I got, the harder he laughed—which upset me more. When we pulled up to the main docks, the Ford car dealer and my dad's best friend were on the dock. They were standing beside a black Lincoln Navigator wrapped in a red bow. I had never seen this type of vehicle before and assumed the dealer was waiting for his wife. When I jumped out of the boat, they all sang "Happy Birthday" to me. I was both excited and confused as I jumped into it. This baby was fully loaded with leather seats, a sunroof, and all the luxuries imaginable. I did not know until later that this gift would be used against me in guilt trips and in future wage negotiations. It was still a great day and I ended up trading the car in for another one a few years later.

What better way to break in a luxury vehicle than to drive it to my timeshare in Orlando? I made the journey from Winnipeg in November, with one of my best friends. When we left, it was minus forty degrees. By the time we made it to Chicago, it was minus twenty, and we kept driving to New Orleans where it was plus twenty-five. The drive took three days and watching the weather get warmer at each stop was thrilling. OutKast's "Hey Ya" became our theme song for the entire trip. We had a friend from Detroit that was going to university in New Orleans, so he hosted us for a couple of days—and what a great host he was. The first night we drove from his house to Bourbon Street in his car, cranking "Hey Ya" and as he was parking, he nailed a parking meter … and nailed it so hard it fell over while also crashing his front tailgate. We were so excited that the damages did not seem to bother any of us. The nightlife of New Orleans was like a giant spring break party. Girls were showing their breasts to trade for beads. Girls were also standing in front of strip clubs, luring men in. I think we may have ventured into one of two of them among many others. I spent the first few days in Orlando with my friend followed by my girlfriend for a week, followed by a friend that drove back home with me.

I should first tell the story of how I met my girlfriend. She was coming to the island lodge to meet my friend the Duke with her girlfriends. I assumed she was coming to see him, as he played for the Manitoba Moose hockey team, and they seemed to have a connection. She brought three friends with her, as some of the guests had asked us to find them some women. Little did they know our little town had hardly any, and especially not a small island like our island lodge. Somehow the Duke pulled it off and they all came. She and I hit it off immediately. After the weekend we continued to see each other.

Chapter 11: The wild and fun times continue.

She lived in Stonewall, Manitoba, so I went to go visit her there during a softball tournament. When she was first at the island lodge, she told me of an ex-boyfriend that was quite physically and emotionally abusive. Crying on my shoulder seemed to be part of what drew her to me. She started crying again at the softball game and showed me a text of him threatening both her and me. I saw him at the bar that night and asked my best friend to have his wife take my girlfriend away, so she didn't have to see me teach him a lesson. I walked up to him at a table and picked him up and threw him against the wall, asking how it feels with someone your own size. The bouncer eventually pulled me off, while they and others bought me drinks outside, thanking me for this. She cried and could not believe I had done this for her honour. We later saw the chief of police at a Winnipeg Blue Bombers game, who thanked me on behalf of the department as they had answered many domestic calls in the past. She was also a massage therapist for the Bombers and had season tickets. We were at this game on my birthday, so she gave me an autographed jersey from the entire team.

We later went to a playoff game against the Saskatchewan team, where it was very cold. I saw an old high-school friend, who approached us and started flirting with her. I was disappointed that she flirted back as they exchanged numbers. She later told me he did not know any girls and she had offered to help him find some another time, so I had nothing to worry about. When I came back from Orlando, he told me they had fooled around, so I had no choice but to end things with her. I mean, I had just been with her in Orlando two weeks before and could not believe they had already made each other's acquaintance in such a short amount of time. One of the girls that came to the island lodge told me later that I was better off, as she had married a man in Thunder Bay and had a child with him within about a year of when we dated. It was too bad how it all ended as we had a lot of fun the times together. I was always skeptical, as any time her name came up around guys, someone would tell me how "they hit her up" or just got her number. Some things in life just are not meant to be.

They say in life we all have a certain type we are attracted to. One night we were in Minneapolis for business and my father decided to treat us to a night out on the city. This was quite unusual for him as he usually likes to do straight business without much fun time in between. A guest at the island lodge that became a friend was a bar back, at a club called Escape, so we decided to head there, and he had us set up with a VIP hostess who met us at the front door. She was a tall, striking blonde with crystal blue eyes that you automatically fell into. My father ordered a bottle of Grey Goose and champagne. I immediately hit it off with this girl and I think she almost blew off the rest of her tables to sit with me more. After we paid our bill, I asked for her number, but she thought my father's executive assistant's personal assistant was my girlfriend. I assured her this girl was a mutual work colleague, so she gave me her number. We spent almost every night together the entire ten days I was in the city. I felt quite love struck for this girl and could tell she felt the same. After the sport show was over each day, she would meet my SOS friends and I at local pubs. They could also all see the instant connection. Myself, my family, and friends all took to her, so she really felt like the one. I was cautiously optimistic because it almost felt too good to be true. I had never felt this strongly about a girl before and she also challenged me intellectually which I was also not used to. The only red flag I could see was that it took her an extremely long time to get ready for almost anything and she had the potential to be a Class A personality. I think that with looks to kill, she was used to getting almost anything she wanted, and I feared being another man of the moment. After I left, we stayed in touch through phone and texts.

My family decided to go to New York for Easter in April. The girl I met in Minneapolis was nicknamed Coley-Bear by her family. I just had to see more of Coley-Bear so I invited her on our trip. She told me her mother thought it might be too quick to go on a family vacation with me, but she was just as excited about our romance as me, so she came. The flight and first day there were great, as we held hands and cuddled the whole time. My father had rooms at the Times Square Marquee

Chapter 11: The wild and fun times continue.

Marriott for all of us, so this added to the excitement. After dinner, she and I went for a walk for ice cream, and everything fell apart. I asked her what age she thought she wanted to be when she got married, and she told me, "Never. And why would I ever want to give myself to one person." I was not asking her this because I anticipated an early marriage, but it felt like she really resented the topic. I was quite heartbroken and felt like I and all we had was just a fun and short-term romance for her. When we got back to the room, she was up all night with the light on so I knew something was wrong, but she would not tell me. My family noticed the instant disconnect and coldness and obviously felt I deserved better treatment than this. My father offered to take us to a New York Yankees baseball game, so she came and was dressed to the nines. We were all in outdoor ballpark gear and she looked like she could go to an award show. Once we got to the game it was chilly, so I offered to get her some gloves. She kept telling me she was fine and to leave her alone, then left the stadium. My uncle was sitting with other girls that he thought would be more fun for me, but I was too distraught and confused at how quickly my current relationship was changing. When we got back to the hotel, she told me she was trying to book a flight home, but all the flights were booked for the holidays. My father talked her into staying and into a better light of mood. This glowing moment lasted only a short time … just until I was called a "boy not a man" because my father had to handle my affairs for me. So, the trip was ruined, and I was confused.

When we got home, I had to see if she had cooled off and kept calling her with no response. Her mother somehow knew what went wrong and called me. She explained that Coley-Bear went cold because they had just found out her father was having an affair which had torn the family apart. Coley-Bear was heartbroken, as they came from a devoted Catholic family. Apparently, this is why she was so dressed up for Easter and now depressed. Her mother explained how much I meant to her, and I should fight to be there for her through this. She promised that it would all be worth it one day, when she realized how much I kept fighting for her. I took this girl to The Mall of America shopping, leased her a new Jeep Cherokee, and kept sending cards and flowers. Finally, almost a year later she saw me in The Escape lounge and said, "Eric, I am fine. Leave me alone and quit sending me things. My mother also needs to butt out." I did not cry with physical tears, but I cried on the inside. I could not believe someone I had such a great start with and felt an instant love for could be so cruel.

When I went to the Duke's wedding in Minneapolis, she met me the day before the wedding. My friend that was a bar back at the Escape brought us out in his boat on Lake Minnetonka as he thought we still had unfinished business. I told her I had a new girlfriend that I thought I would eventually marry. (And did!) At this time, I did not know I would marry her, but Coley-Bear's reactions surprised me. When we got back, she hugged and kissed me saying, "That girl is so lucky, my mother will never forgive me as I try to forgive myself." I knew then that she had always loved me, but I guess her heart just was not ready at the time. Her mother apologized to me later for pushing a relationship that was obviously not ready to fully develop. But it was not all lost, as I still call her mother my Minneapolis Mom and have a special connection to that family. I have never heard an explanation from this girl. Her mother has apologized on both their be halves for putting the daughter's feelings above mine and what that must have put my emotions through. I can only presume the daughter felt the same as me but was afraid to open the door, but I have never been told that—so it's a scar that's left from the past.

It seems the "Minni Apple" of Minneapolis is where I spent most of my time during the sport show season, so in and around that area sit many of my memories. There was a gentleman's club that I was very fond of and of course a girl I became quite attracted to. I always made a point of visiting this club at least once during any show I was at in the area. She was quite famous in the club and a classy young woman. Her looks and the way she held herself to higher moral standards made her stand out quite a bit. Her dancing name was also the same as one

Chapter 11: The wild and fun times continue.

of my grandmothers so that gave us one connection. She also grew up on the US side of The Lake of The Woods which is the same lake our family resorts are located giving us another connection. Many dancers get into this profession as single mothers, to support their children, while others support their bad habits. This girl was using the money to put herself through school to be a massage therapist. Who would have thought an exotic dancer could be the girl I would most come to admire? I always thought she was out of my league, so I conducted myself as a gentleman and minded my boundaries. I think my gentleman qualities won her over and we started to date. Her connections in the club brought many great things. Men would give her VIP tickets and expensive dinner vouchers hoping this would lead to a date with them, but she saved them to enjoy with me. I mean, talk about a friend with benefits! I also became friends with other employees of the club as the DJ would play "O Canada" or announce, "Canada is now in the house." The house-mom that took care of the girls would come up to visit me. They also asked me to judge new potential dancers on amateur night. These were girls hoping to win the grand prize as well as a job in the future. I gained quite the stature in this facility. The one memory that stands out is getting offered to come to Prince's rave after the bars closed. Yes, that is correct—the famous Minnesota performer Prince, from the *Purple Rain* movie. He did not appear at his party, but it was in his garage with many high-performance cars that were covered over. There was also a personal bartender and a large fish tank with exotic fish. Some of his pictures and concert memorabilia were in there to validate this was his palace. There is a bar called First Avenue that he owned after his *Purple Rain* movie was shot there. The first date she and I had together was in this club. This girl came to visit me a few times on and off during our fishing season. It is hard for me to admit that I could break up with a girl this astounding. Customers of the resort would recognize her and make offers for private dances at the lodge and to come back on the bus with them. This was so highly disrespectful to both her and me that I think I imploded. I was also young and I think my emotions caught the best of me. We both moved on into other life ventures but remain close friends to this day. Most relationships end with hurt feelings and disappointment but I this is one of the few that ended well.

I never thought of myself as a driving machine, but I have had my experiences with "long hauls." The taxidermist and I left Winnipeg at about 5 a.m. in very sub-zero temperatures and drove straight through to Chicago which was about fourteen hours. We went out with the Sky Vodka rep, which left us not enough rest the next day. We still got up and 6 a.m. and drove the rest of the way to New Orleans. After a couple of days with our "Hey Ya" host, we drove to Orlando to my timeshare for more great adventures. I had another friend that joined after he left and we drove from Orlando to Chicago, after being up the night before. We had no cash for pay tolls and my credit card limit on ATMs was maxed out. It was very interesting navigating through the Illinois pay tolls. Once we found a hotel, we checked in and slept for two days straight before getting up to drive the rest of the way home. I think we both needed a sleeping vacation after that drive.

There was a bar in downtown Orlando on Church Street called Mako's. I quickly became a known regular in there. The female bartenders would wear lingerie while the males wore kilts and no shirts. Every hour on the hour after 10 p.m. was a black out. The lights would go out, with the DJ coming onto the stage singing Disturbed's "Down with the Sickness." There were paper napkins being shot around with what became a white out. Bartenders and shooter girls offered free shots to pump up the energy. Most of the bartenders knew me by name, so patrons thought I was part owner of the club. With the amount of money, I spent in there, I must have had shares that I should be asking about. It is to my understanding the club has since closed because of behaviour that went on later.

On my way back from Wisconsin to Minnesota, I used to stop into Eau Claire, Wisconsin. A friend of mine from high school was going to the university there. He was two years younger than me and had

Chapter 11: The wild and fun times continue.

acquired a hockey scholarship. It was always entertaining to visit him, and his hockey team mates while I was in for the night. As I always came late Saturday or Sunday, the bars and streets were not very busy. These guys came to like me so much from my visits that they decided to book a trip to the island lodge one summer. I never intended for my visits to turn into sales for the resort but sometimes the best business comes from sincere intentions.

They came up in June on a father-and-sons Father's Day trip. As with most guests, they wanted me to take them into Kenora one night, so I obliged. They were a little disappointed in the lack of available women but enjoyed the boat trip each way. My friend the Duke from the English Hockey League also found us in the busiest local bar, called Haps. When I was outside rounding these fellows up to head home, something happened I will never forget. A young fellow with a shaved head came running across the understand what had just happened. By the time I came to, the Duke had already put him in his place. But talk about picking the wrong guy on the wrong night! The hockey guys saw me with a bloody nose and grabbed the fellow to also put him in his place. To this day I have no idea who that was or why he came running across the lot, but I am quite sure he must have learned some sort of lesson. I can only presume drugs and alcohol intoxicated his better judgement that night. On a brighter note, I maintained a relationship with most of the hockey guys for quite some time after they stayed there.

To this day, my favorite guest at the island lodge was a gentleman from the Minnesota and Wisconsin border. He is a huge Green Bay Packers fan, thus part of our connection. He liked me so much that he offered me tickets to join him in the box suites he had at a Packers game in November. I could not believe the difference of experience in these suites. He had food and beverages catered while we were in there. We played against the Atlanta Falcons on a cold day, which made the experience inside even better. My friends teased me about being a tootsie boy up in the boxes, but I knew they were just jealous. To be honest I did kind of miss the comradery of being with the fans outside cheering, so he showed me the seats just outside the box where we could sit. But like I said, it was quite cold, so the outside experience wore off quickly enough and I came back into the promise land. Walking in and around the stadium with that ticket around my neck was quite the surreal feeling.

The best basketball game I have ever been to must be The Milwaukee Bucks. The vice president of Miller Brewing was a major sponsor of the team and had courtside tickets. He would drop these tickets off for us at our hotel so we could go to the game. The head chef from the main lodge was with us the one year I got these tickets. I remember him as the most versatile chef any of the resorts has ever had, because he would also do boat runs in the summer and sport shows in the winter. A player flying off the court landed almost right into us and spilled chef's beer right into his lap. He laughed and said he did not care because he got the beer dumped on him by an NBA player. I was glad that he did not care because I was afraid to admit that I also did not care. It was on our way to a game that I saw Brett Favre jump into the elevator ahead of me.

CHAPTER 12:
The years that ended bachelor life into engagement

Throughout my twenties I always knew I did not want to get married until I was at least thirty years old. I witnessed many of my friends and colleagues get married after high school then watched separations happen quickly afterwards. There appears to be a pressure society puts on us after our college years are completed. It is common to hear such questions and statements: "When are you going to find a serious relationship?" "Isn't it time to get married now?" "When do you plan to buy a house and have children?" "Your biological clock is ticking." I knew I had a lot in life to explore before I decided to commit to one person for the rest of my life.

Then all the sudden, without me knowing or expecting it, along came "The One." My father decided to sponsor a company staff outing at the local golf course. My friend Coolie brought two girls from the island lodge location to join us. One girl was the sister of a long-time bartender who I think was intended to be set up with me. The other was a girl named EM, who was also a sister of a long-time server. I bought some hats and shirts so we could form a team unity. I ordered Playboy gear as that seemed fun and cute. EM immediately told me she had heard about my reputation, and this would only be friendly. I really thought she did not like me at all from how cold she initially was. After a couple of holes and beverages she started to warm up to me and I could feel the "soft eyes" coming out. By the end of the course, she was sitting on my lap. Because everyone had been drinking, they decided to stay the night instead of heading back to the island lodge. This felt like an excuse to stay with me. And who am I to refuse such a fitting excuse?

Throughout the summer we ended up spending quite a bit of time together. Boat rides ended up with me staying at the island lodge or she with me the main lodge. She told me she originally came to the island lodge to escape an ex-boyfriend that was giving her a hard time. By the end of the summer, she accepted a year-round position at the main lodge as a reservation's coordinator. I was a little apprehensive about this, as my father oversaw reservations and my sister also worked in there. Just as I feared, my family made her feel quite unwelcome, so I felt her agony all through the winter.

That summer, the tensions continued to build. We moved into the guest cabin at my father's island. He claimed to have invested quite a bit to spruce it up for us. We appreciated the gesture, but it was still quite small. This cabin had one bedroom with a spare room that we used for storage and one small bathroom. We appreciated the scenery on the lake at night but felt we had almost no privacy. My father walked by our cabin on his way to his boat for work. He would make comments about what he would see us doing as he walked by. One day he kicked in my door, yelling at me that I must be hungover as I was still not at work. Although I was ill with a cold, I had already been to and from work. Apparently, he did not see me go by his place in my boat and assumed I had been out all night. The tensions throughout the summer got to be unbearable so we decided to leave the resort to move to British Columbia.

My friend Bizzy's girlfriend's parents owned a house in Kelowna. They refurbished the basement into a one-bedroom apartment they rented out for extra income. They were in Mexico for the winter and

Chapter 12: The years that ended bachelor life into engagement

the current tenant was moving out. Bizzy told us the rent, which seemed quite high, but it included utilities and cable TV, so we decided to take it. When the landlords returned, they barely said hello to us. They felt the rent was too low—the past tenant had been a friend. They had never been happy with the previous rent amount and proclaimed that Bizzy should not have offered this rate to us. They decided the first and last month rent should be used for the months that were too low. This obviously made us feel quite uncomfortable in the situation. They also said we should live as quietly as possible, so that they would almost not know we were there, and we were not to use the backyard or any of their belongings. I quickly realized this was not the friendly rental we were promised.

Before coming to the island lodge, EM had gone on a backpacking trip through Europe and South America with some girlfriends. She explained this trip had been quite the exotic romping for everyone except her. I did not realize they already had a deposit down on another trip. Her friends told her that if she did not come, their friendship was over—so she packed up and left. I was not in favour of this whole idea from the picture she painted of the past trip. Her friends said I sounded like a control freak, so she bolted. I was now left with a high rent to pay on my own. I sensed a pattern, as she also told me she had left her last boyfriend for the island lodge … and now I was also abandoned. Once she got back to Ontario, she immediately called me, crying, saying she had made a big mistake. Her friends were cruel, and she missed the man she loved. I was hesitant about taking her back but appreciated her humility in the matter. She came back and on went the Kelowna adventures.

I spent time looking at restaurant properties to purchase or vacant premises to open a new restaurant. I ended up in a deal with a man who was not a restaurant entrepreneur but had taken a restaurant over—the business next to his cigar bar—when it foreclosed. The restaurant had a bad feel, with a potential partner I did not feel much trust in, so my plans for that vanished. I later decided to try selling door-to-door vacuums with a company called Kirby. We literally knocked door to door, offering people free shampoo samples so we could give a two-hour presentation. I learned quite a bit about human psychology from the training they gave us. We went on the road for five-day trips throughout Alberta and BC, bunking five people in small rooms. I became quite good at the selling portion once inside a house, but knocking on doors was not for me. After being told off for the last time, I went to a bus station to go home. I grabbed a bottle of whiskey in the depot store and drank away the end of my door-selling days.

After the restaurant project and sales adventures did not work out, we had quite the fun summer. I was looking for a new career and we realized this was not a good city to start out in life. Kelowna is really a great city, with scenic views of Lake Okanagan and a close drive to the Big White ski mountain. You could literally ski in the morning, drive back down the hill and kayak in the afternoon. There are fresh fruit stands at each corner as well as wineries all over the lake. EM worked at one called Mission Hill that had an exquisite restaurant patio. She also had some friends from Southern Ontario that came out to live close to us. I can say this was one of the most fun summers I have ever had. I had never had the opportunity to enjoy a summer as I was usually working nonstop.

Unfortunately, all the good times came with a high financial price. As my career ventures were not working out, I was spending a large amount of my savings so we could survive. When I asked my father's assistant for help with buying new furniture, they sent me a $500 gift certificate. This did not go far in furnishing our home. This was a clear message from him, telling us off for leaving. I had a truck that was paid for by the company for work and was informed those payments had ended. I had actually traded in a birthday-present vehicle for this company car so I was left in a lurch.

Although the financial pressures grew, so did our love and connection. I remember the day I proposed to her. We were arguing about our expenses, so I staged a huge fight. I left her crying and upset, knowing I

Chapter 12: The years that ended bachelor life into engagement

would have a big surprise she would never expect when she got home. I went to the jewelry store to purchase a diamond engagement ring. When she came home, I had the lights dimmed low with soft music playing. I gave her a card—which she assumed was an apology—that was my proposal. I put the ring in the glass of champagne she was drinking. I guess she did not clue into all of this … she almost drank the ring as she pounded down the bubbly. Once she saw the ring and read the note again, she cried. I took the tears as a yes, so we were officially engaged.

My father, sister, and brother came for a visit and convinced us to move back. They had learned a lesson with me being gone and pleaded for our return. We packed all our things to return home to the family estate once again.

CHAPTER 13:
Marriage and birth of a new child

We moved home and back onto the island's guest cabin. After a short amount of time, it was quite clear that nothing had changed, and the turmoil was back on. My father was already blaming me for things I was not a part of. Although I was not there to make decisions, he concluded things had gone poorly because I ran away instead of sticking it out like a man. Ultimately every problem that had happened over the previous year was somehow still my fault. This felt unfair as there were decisions made that I would not have made and did not agree with.

My sister was also quite unfriendly to EM. My sister was engaged to a young man who had thrown the ring at her during a fight. She cried and said yes, so this apparently turned into the proposal. EM and my sister worked on marriage invitations together. EM was so happy that my sister was so helpful with this. EM found out later that our invites were sent from Canada with regular post while my sister overnight expressed hers from the USA. Apparently, since our wedding was first, my sister wanted my family to receive her invitations before ours so she would get the first commitments. My sister was also quite jealous that EM's ring was nicer than hers and treated her like a gold-digger with constant comments about it.

Chapter 13: Marriage and birth of a new child

Our return did not last long before we knew we had to leave once again. During a visit to EM's hometown a sister cried, asking why everyone had to move so far away and saying that a family should stay closer together. EM and I decided to move to Richmond Hill in the suburbs of Toronto to be closer to the family.

After much searching around for apartments, we found a basement apartment from a nice Italian family. They seemed to have enough money to let the daughter stay upstairs on her own while we rented the basement. They put a lot of work into the apartment to make it more comfortable. They also made us feel quite welcome to use the garage, backyard, and dogs' play pen. We felt much more comfortable here that the Kelowna experience.

I filed for unemployment insurance and realized the Greater Toronto area can be quite cold. I applied for many jobs and was often shot down before being given a fair interview. Once again, I was left spending savings while I searched for a new career. EM found a job in social services as that was her education and work experience. She seemed content in these positions, but they do not offer much for compensation which left me with most of the expenses.

After spending most of the winter looking for a job, I was finally offered a position in Wasaga Beach for The Park Bridge corporation at their Country Life Resorts. This resort had a RV park, retirement community mobile home area, as well as a cottage land-leased area. There were three resorts in one premise, making this their most complicated resort to operate. The president informed me he offered me this position to monitor my progress. He felt I was a good candidate for an area manager of multiple resorts.

The contracts tenants signed were quite detailed, with a large binder agreement. Learning the complexities of three land-leased operations came with a huge learning curve. I was given little to no training, as the past manager was promoted to another area and his temporary fill-in was more of a handy man on operations. As I was being looked at for the area manager position, I was the only resort manager, with no area manager to direct me. This was the president's first resort acquisition, so he decided to be my temporary area manager until I was ready to take on the promotion.

He was a Polish man who had started with three resorts in Wasaga Beach. He had kept acquiring, building, and expanding resorts until he and his partners formed a corporation. When I was there, it had expanded to approximately fifty resorts in Ontario. He was an extremely hard man to work for. I noticed a hostile work environment with quick turnovers. My gut feeling told me I might not last long.

EM and I bought a house in Wasaga Beach. Even though it felt like a hostile work environment, we knew it was best to create a home. She also wanted to start a family, so having a home was the smartest idea. EM found a position at the local YMCA which also did not provide much income. This left me to pay most of the bills.

It is an amazing thing when a woman wants to breed a child how quickly it can happen. Soon upon trying we were pregnant right away. Unfortunately, as soon as we found out, she had a miscarriage … We learned that this is quite a common thing on the first pregnancy as the women's womb isn't always ready and the body has not prepared for the significant changes that are about to come. After a month or two of rest we were once again pregnant and this time the little bambino stayed healthy. I was mostly excited but also a little nervous, as this was really going to happen. Doctors informed us that there are three trimesters and the things we should prepare for in each. I was mostly told to be supportive and patient, as the mother is the one dealing with the physical duress. I like to feel that I was both, but in the third trimester I was treated otherwise. Our relationship had taken a total change, leaving me feeling I could do no right. Other fathers told me this was normal with the change in hormones, and that a few months after childbirth things would go back to normal. I must disagree because we were no longer equals and from the six-month period until the day, we divorced I could do nothing right. My uncle is a psychologist and informed me this is common after a miscarriage because mothers tend to blame

Chapter 13: Marriage and birth of a new child

themselves. Even though it feels like I am getting the blame, the mother is under constant stress of losing another child.

EM made a deal with me that we could call out child Leo Masters IV, if he was identified by the middle name, so he could have his own identity while carrying on my family name. She also felt it was fair for her to o pick the name if it was a girl. I agreed, so every morning and night I prayed for a healthy baby boy.

I remember the day he was born like it was yesterday. It was a full moon, meaning the gravity has a larger pull. Apparently, this is when most births happen each month. We were sent back and forth several times until EM had dilated enough to get an open delivery room, my son was a complicated birth to say the least. The nurses where short-handed from all the deliveries happening so I was put on EM's back to help push him out. I can only imagine the duress she must have been under because I was sweating like I just ran a marathon. The mixed emotions and excitement that happen when you finally get to meet your child are almost unexplainable. I could see why many fathers faint, as I struggled to hold my feet on the ground. That carrying and giving birth to my son was the best gift EM could have ever given to me. To this day I am still grateful every minute I get to spend with him.

The relationship at my workplace in Wasaga Beach went from bad to even worse. I think part of the reason I was hired is because the president was interested in taking my family's businesses over as a new acquisition in northern Ontario. He suggested that he, his father, and I should take a trip to the resort at his expense. I explained why this could not happen due to the falling out I'd had at home. After this I went from hero to zero; it felt like I was just another liability instead of a potential asset.

The cabins were owned by the tenants that purchased them. Several of the owners entered a rental pool program. Rental revenue was split between the tenants for owning them and the resort for managing the program. I walked by one of the rentals with a U-Haul van parked in front of it and blankets all over the windows. It appeared new people might have been moving in, so I thought of knocking to welcome them. I decided that could wait for another day as they could use some privacy. On Monday, the contracted housekeeper asked me to come to the cabin immediately. I was surprised, as she had previously never asked me to rush over so quickly. Upon entry to the cabin, I quickly saw why she felt it was so urgent for me to see the scene. It appeared that someone had opened a can of varsal paint thinner and dumped them all over the walls, sink drains, bathtub, and toilets. It took me a moment to accept this was really happening. The office manager informed me the customers had insisted on paying cash instead of by credit card and had paid double to do so. She had called the owners of the cabin and they had agreed to this because they wanted the extra revenue. I thought perhaps the renters had hard feelings with the owners and had purposely left no trace when they destroyed their cabin. I called the police, and they sent the DNA unit. They informed me we should not have been in the cabin or touched anything as it had been turned into a crystal meth lab. Everything in the cabin was now toxic, meaning no one should be in there without masks and gloves. Coming from a small town in northern Ontario, I thought this only happened on television and could not believe this was for real. The cabin instantly became a criminal investigation site with yellow tape all around it. The police estimated that over one million dollars of meth was made in this cabin, and that they had dumped the remains down all the sink drains. The walls were residue from cooking. I had to call the vice president who told me to remove myself and not to answer any questions from the media. I was happy to do as I was told, as the less I had to do with this mess the better.

 The cottage units are considered recreational and not permanent residential. Tenants paid less in taxes due to this, but some tried to stay permanently. The corporation had to implement a water shutdown period two times per year to force the tenants out. I had to patrol the property to ensure no one was on sight during these three-to-four-week periods. This period made me quite an unpopular man. Tenants

Chapter 13: Marriage and birth of a new child

in each section fought with each other quite frequently. Vacation properties are supposed to be an escape from your day-to-day problems. But some brought their at-home city drama to the resort. I chalk this up to human drama.

I remember my exit from this company quite well. The president asked me to come to the sales office to have a meeting with him in approximately half an hour. The sales office was in the recreation hall and banquet area. I decided to head over early to check up on the facilities. The health inspector was quite strict on the bacteria vs. chlorine levels in the hot tub and pool. We also had teenagers that liked to cause destruction to these facilities, amongst other areas in the resort. To my delight the pH levels were perfect, and the pool area was in perfect order. The banquet hall had not been utilized in quite some time, so it was also in perfect order. I decided it would be a good idea to pay a visit to the sales manager before my meeting with the president. We had to have many meetings as sales and resort operations cross paths in their sales pitches. The sales manager was busy talking to clients, so I went to the waiting area. The president was in this area eating lunch. He was quite upset as he felt I was disturbing his private lunch time. He said, "I told you to meet me in thirty minutes, but I guess you were sitting in your office with your thumbs up your ass so came running right over." I was quite appalled with his reaction but maintained my composure, stayed calm, and explained my property check on the way over. He said I could quit kissing his ass and give him some privacy while he ate in peace. Thankfully the sales manager was finished with his meeting, so I went to sit with him while chief finished eating. I knew by the initial temperature of the president's tone this was not going to be a pleasant meeting. The sales manager chuckled and said this is quite common—when he has bad days, he takes it out on his subordinates—and encouraged me not to take it personally.

The president came in to grab me and informed me this was not a meeting but an inspection tour. He had me come into his car to do a tour of the property. He picked apart every single detail. I could tell the sales manager was correct that my boss was having a bad day and needed to unload on me. I left the car, went home, slept, then woke up and wrote him an email describing how inappropriate his behaviour towards me and most of the employees was. I felt like Jerry Maguire writing his company mission statement. I was not only defending myself but each person I saw subjected to this behavior in the company.

The human resources director, who had also been part of hiring me, called me over for a meeting in the morning. She took the opportunity to brown nose him by putting me down. The president straight out asked me if I would like to stay working for him or leave. While also informing me the promotion was off the table and I would need to be thankful for his mercy. His tone was much like Caesar in *Gladiator* asking his sister "Am I not merciful?". I told him I needed no mercy or grace and it's best I leave the company now. He said, "I do not know if this is me firing you or you are quitting but I guess it does not matter." I said we both knew exactly what this was and walked out with my head held high. I mean, how many people get to tell the torrent of a boss off?!

My wife knew all the duress the position had put me under, so I was disappointed in her discouraging attitude. Perhaps I was relieved to be away from this toxic environment, but she was worried about our finances as I was the significant breadwinner.

After a short amount of time off, I accepted a position as a timeshare sales associate at the Georgian Manor Resort in Collingwood, Ontario. This was approximately a fifteen-minute drive from our house in Wasaga Beach. And yes, I really was the guy sitting at the desk convincing you that you are going to spend $50-$250,000 today. I own a timeshare in Orlando, Florida, so this made me a natural fit. I learned even more about human psychology from the tours I gave. For anyone that likes to travel every year, it really is a great investment. For people just looking for a free night stay to take the tour, it is not going to be a good experience. I realized the high pressure us commission salesmen are put under. No sale means no pay. The more you sell the more tours you get. I sold more of the highest packages in my three months than

Chapter 13: Marriage and birth of a new child

any other salesperson in history. More in three months than most do in a year. The financial pressure was too high, so I had to quit. I had proved everything I needed to myself, and it was time to get back into business management. Once again, my wife was not in favour of this decision, but I have always been confident in my abilities to execute my goals and challenges.

After my shot at timeshares, I was unemployed for a very short amount of time. Friends I had met in the timeshares had me trying to sell hot-water tanks door to door. I was quite reluctant to try this as two times in commission sales had already burned buy out. On the third day of canvassing, I was literally saved by the bell with a phone call. A resort I had applied for in British Columbia had a recruiter call me while I was walking. The resort was called Gibson's Pass Inc., operating for Manning Park Resort. This was a family-owned company that had been forced into bankruptcy. The bank in British Columbia hired a receivership company based out of Vancouver. This company hired a recruiting firm to acquire a new general manager to resurrect the property into a profitable standing.

I was both flattered and nervous to be called about such an adventure. They offered to pay for my flight to tour the property and interview with the head receiver of the project. This resort was a ski hill in the winter and based on BC's largest provincial park. This establishment also had a bundle package to oversee quite a few parks within a one-hundred-kilometer distance. The core of the resort had a full-service main lodge with a restaurant, bar, and two levels of hotel rooms. There were also approximately six cabins around the main lodge area. I could tell this would be a very complicated project to take on. There was also staff accommodation across the highway where most of the resort's employees lived. There were quite a few similarities to my family's operations, as it was quite remote with all the employees living on site. I could instantly tell why they wanted to recruit me for this challenge. Apparently, the current general manager was brought on short term to pave the way for the future General Manager. The operations manager is the man I spent most of my onsite tour with. He was an older gentleman, semi-retired, and seemed quite wealthy. This gentleman and the head recruiter were friends and neighbors on the Whistler Mountain area.

After a three-day tour of the resorts and area, the recruiting firm instantly saw me as a match and offered me the position. The position guaranteed me compensation for one year's salary with a sizable bonus as an incentive to bring it back to a profitable state. The offer was too good to refuse so I instantly called my wife back in Ontario. She had already been looking at the website and jumped for joy. I went back to the head recruiter, accepted the position, and signed a contract. The contract was guaranteed for one year with a second-year option. It appeared they were optimistic I could bring the resort back to good standing in the first year. The second-year option was to help the receivership company sell the property once the books were back in order. The bank's primary concern was getting their two-million-dollar debt recovered.

My wife found a log cabin in Hope, BC, which was an approximate one-hour drive from the resort. We signed a rental agreement lease to stay there. I drove our Mazda car while a moving company transported all our goods to this cabin. My wife flew to meet me in Hope. The cabin was gorgeous and like something off a real-estate television show. Unfortunately, the commute to and from the resort each day was too much so we cancelled our lease and moved to the resort. Part of the compensation for the general manager was a modular home in the employee residence area. This was a two bedroom that all three of us could reside in. The unit was small but saved us quite a bit of money as all utilities were also included in my compensation package.

Once I started my position, I could instantly tell what a desperate despair the operation had fallen into. As the last regime was in the progress of going bankrupt, all the facilities had diminished. Many of the long-time employees quit because they did not like the new changes brought on with the receivership program. Employees that

Chapter 13: Marriage and birth of a new child

stayed on were hostile as they were loyal to the past family who they felt had been pushed out. The resort had no financial credibility, so the operation manager was paying everything on his credit card. Once the resort gained some finances, the controller paid him back. I realized the operations manager had a master's degree in business accounting, so he worked closely with the controller on our financial reports. I sometimes felt left in the dark, as they were always together.

As I was left in a hostile environment, I had to make many changes with the organics of the company. The current controller was retired and had no desire to stay on, so I hired a junior person to relieve her position. This was a young Filipino man out of university with no prior experiences with a head controller position. This was a new experience for both of us. The current ski hill manager was an alcoholic that had been harassing some of the ski hill employees, so I had to terminate him. The current assistant to the operations manager was also from a small camp on the other side of BC. She had never worked in a complex resort, so I also had to inform her that her services were no longer required. I could tell that even though the receivership company had made this decision before my arrival, it came as a complete surprise and disappointment to her. We also did not have a human resource or recruiting department. My wife had previous HR experience with her social services as well as resort experience, so I hired her for this position. In quite a clumsy and awkward way it was best that we parted ways with the past regime and formed a new management team, so we had a fresh start. The only person that stayed on was the operation manager as he was paying most of the bills.

British Columbia Parks had a supervisor that came to inspect us at least once per week. He was quite involved with the operations of the park bundles, with an interest in over seeing how we managed them. Manning Park Resort and BC Park had an extensive contract that was signed to ensure this park kept the standards of all BC parks. This was a large undertaking. The operations manager handled this duty while I oversaw all the executive level functions.

I was hired as the general manager but resumed vice president duties. The resort did not have an owner, president, or acting CEO, so I assumed these duties. The bank required a ten-to-twenty-page report each month. This report was to include the budget vs. actual income statements with a detailed explanation of the operations. It appeared the bank had hired the receivership company to act as the board of directors. I worked for the bank but reported to the receivership company on their behalf. As all the facilities assets had eroded, I had the challenge of rebuilding them with little to no budget. Over the year we rebuilt the ski lifts, painted cabins, refurbished buildings—and all while managing daily operations in each department. I felt lucky to have so many department managers as I had to trust them to maintain their areas while I focused on my executive level management duties.

The resorts also did not have a sales manager or IT department, so I recruited a company out of Vancouver—this was a husband-and-wife team that each specialized in the two areas. These two billed us as a consultant fee. As the phones, computers, and internet had all collapsed, I needed to rebuild these. The husband gave me an expensive quote to rebuild all of this. I was put in a tough position as I knew we could not afford this much money but needed new restructure. My wife had a college friend that was a partner in an IT firm based out of Ontario, so we called him up. After my wife called her friend, he flew to our resort to look at our needs, offer advice, and give a quote. Let's call this fellow Slick Nick as he was quite slick. He was well polished, groomed, and wore nice clothes. He offered a solution that was a lot less than the consultants out of Vancouver, so I accepted his quote. He informed me he required a fifty percent deposit to order all the hardware and software, so we accepted. The resort was now making enough money to write a check instead of the operation manager putting it on this credit card. We had also rebuilt our credibility with all the suppliers, so he was off the hook on a personal level.

Quite honestly, I enjoyed rebuilding the structure, integrity, and reputation of the resort. It was an endless challenge, but business

Chapter 13: Marriage and birth of a new child

always feels like my background calling. The town of Hope asked me to sit on their board of city directors. I accepted this position and came to monthly meetings. Hope and Manning Park seemed to have a long-standing relationship and they welcomed me with open arms.

Slick Nick returned with all his supplies to resurrect our IT structures. I could not help but notice he looked completely different. The well-polished man in nice clothes was now in dirty and baggy clothes. I assumed this was because the sales part was over and now he needed to stay comfortable getting down to work. He requested to do his work at night, so he did not disturb our office operations during the day. This seemed quite reasonable, so we accepted the request.

My wife was very excited to see Slick Nick as he was an old college friend. She felt we could not associate with the employees as I was their boss, and she oversaw the human resources. She said she would like to go over to see him, to keep him company while he did his work. Even though a part of me was skeptical of this being a distraction to his work, I did not have the heart to decline. After all, "a happy wife is a happy life." I made her a deal that if she put our newborn son to bed so I could sleep, this was cool with me. She agreed and quickly fled. I noticed when she came back that she wreaked like red wine. She proclaimed that Slick Nick brought back some wine from his last IT contract. Apparently Slick Nick flew all over North and South America for these IT projects. I was now informed that he was a single man that loved the adventures of travelling. Night after night, my wife kept coming home more intoxicated. The wine turned into hard liquor and the tequilas he brought back from other places. This upset me, both as the husband, the father of our child, and as general manager of the resort. She was now coming in late and changing her work schedule around his. I explained how unacceptable this was on all levels. Things went from bad to worse!

Slick Nick explained he had finished all he could for now and needed to come back to finish the rest when he had more supplies. He also needed another twenty-five percent to order the rest of what he needed. My operations manager saw what was going on with my wife so sat him down for a lecture. He asked this fellow to send the bills for the supplies he needed as we could not give him any more money until the job was completed. Slick Nick kept sizing me up as thought I was competition instead of a customer. I was quite a bit larger than him, so stayed away and let my operations manager deal with h

My wife and I went back to Collingwood, Ontario, for her sister's wedding. As soon as we got there, I felt an awkward tension with her. I assumed this was from the excitement of seeing her friends and family as well as the nervousness of the wedding. I was later informed her mother had to talk her into coming back with me, as she said she was not happy. I had no idea of any of this, as we were trying to conceive a second child. The resort was also in much better shape, and I was a few months away from getting my incentive bonus. Yes, we had our disagreements as all couples with newborn children do. But all in all, I felt it was a successful marriage.

After sister Chloe's wedding we returned to Manning Park and so did Slick Nick. He was gone for a couple of weeks, and I noticed he was quite a bit larger now. This fellow had obviously started working out and found some illegal steroids to help him. My experience with exercise tells me that no one gets this big this quick. I could tell he was trying to outdo me. Now instead of just going to the office to see him at night, they were making plans outside of the resort. My wife went with him to another resort. I was already upset that we had hired a nanny, as she was not into her motherly or work duties. She called me from this resort to inform me they had been drinking and would be staying the night. I could not believe she intended to spend a night with another man while I was at the resort with our eighteen-month baby. She blamed it on me and I could hear Slick Nick in the background talking about what a control freak I was. When she got back, I tried to explain this guy was a homewrecker and going after the one he couldn't get in college. Unfortunately, I felt like I was talking to a different person as I was now the bad guy.

Chapter 13: Marriage and birth of a new child

I purchased a Jeep Cherokee as it was better equipped to drive in the mountains than my past CUV. The receivership company said the last family's son had a Toyota 4Runner. He was the operations manager and had this vehicle as part of his compensation. As the resort went bankrupt, the bank seized his vehicle. The receivership told me that it was now mine to drive as part of my compensation. It is a very well-built truck and felt like the toughest vehicle I had ever been in.

My wife decided that living on the mountain was no longer fun and decided to move to Vancouver. She found a small apartment there. She felt that because I had the 4Runner it was best for her to drive the Jeep back and forth to Vancouver. Her three to four days a week at the resort turned into two or three. She came up and stayed in a resort hotel room while there. She was bragging to staff how much fun the big city was and that she had met a new boyfriend. The environment of the entire resort was now deflated. My wife hired these people in human resources but worked for me in operations. They could also see my hurt so sided with me.

At about this very time my one-year contract was coming to an end. The receivership asked me to submit my one-year report and forecast for next year. After I submitted this, they asked me to come to Vancouver for a meeting. When I assumed the position, the resort had been losing over $300,000 per year. Monday, I drove down to Vancouver to meet the receivership CEO and vice president. I assumed they were going to congratulate me for turning a $250,000 profit in the first year, which is over a half a million-dollar turnaround. I also assumed we would strategize about next year's budget forecast. This was far from the meeting's agenda. They explained that $250,000 for the first year was mildly acceptable as I had to learn new things but the $350,000 budget for next year was nowhere near acceptable. They explained that the bank wanted their two million back immediately, with no desire to wait two to four years with my budgets. I explained the resort needs to keep its integrity and reputation, but this was of no interest to them. I left with a lump in my throat, knowing I was now too expensive for them and that my position and salary was the easiest to cut. My bonus was also based on incentives, with no actual figure at the signing of my contract, leaving it to their interpretation. I really got a taste of the corporate dog-eat-dog environment.

When my wife came back to the resort, I explained the outcome of my meeting and she rolled her eyes, saying I was always just too worried. I could not believe her lack of care or concern. I realized she had other interests and was probably already looking for new jobs to mesh with her new life in Vancouver.

A week after my meeting, the head recruiter surprised me with an unannounced meeting. This meeting turned out to be an onsite inspection. I could tell he was looking for reasons to terminate my contract. Most of what he said made no sense, especially for a retired man that had not been there the entire time I was. He could not even look me in the eye on leaving, when I shook his hand. He and my operations manager spent the afternoon on the ski hill, so I instantly smelled a rat. Within a few days, the vice president of the recruiting company came up to inform me my services were no longer required. He must have been concerned about my reaction as he brought two others with him. The VP had one man beside him at my desk while the other stood outside my door. He also informed me that my vice president would be taking over my position and I had one week to vacate the premises. My visions of the past meeting came true. He also informed me that I had one month left on my contract and half the bonus would be my severance.

I could not believe how much my life had changed within a two-month span.

CHAPTER 14:
The restart of a new life as a bachelor

Vegas! Vegas! Vegas! With my career on the ski hill over and my wife moved to Vancouver I was in great despair. What else could I do but ask two of my best friends to join me in Las Vegas? This trip would soon be known as My Divorce Party. Coincidentally, the Rook and Wisconsin Badger that cleaned the money at my wedding party were the two that came along. Luckily, I had a two-bedroom condo from my timeshare in Orlando, so we traded to head there. The Badger was not happy because our condo was at the very far end of the strip, past Circus Circus hotel. Each time we went back to the prime area of the strip it was at least a twenty-five-dollar taxi ride and equally as long in minutes. Our room was also right beside the outdoor pool, which was under construction. The Badger was agitated by waking up to sledgehammers each morning followed by a lengthy ride to the strip. The Rookie and I did not care, as we had better things to do than spend too much time in the condo. Quite honestly, I was just glad to be out of the hostile environment at the ski hill and away from the aggregation of my wife. You find out who your best friends are when your life is in turmoil, and these two gentlemen are them.

These two had arrived before me so I met them at Larry Flints Hustlers Club. They had two girls anxiously awaiting my arrival. All I know is, dancers sure know how to boost a man's ego back up. I wished my buddies were waiting at the club I'd had my bachelor party at. I wanted to see if the Columbian girl who had warned me about marrying a Canadian was still there. The Badger assured me that she had found another American to marry and get her visa with. He was most likely correct, but I would still like to have seen what she said.

We had so many fun adventures on this trip. The first that comes to mind is getting kicked out of the Palms Casino for being too loud. We were the only ones on the main floor, with all of us winning. The Badger presumed they were upset to be giving us winnings, so we headed up to the Playboy Lounge. The Rookie brought me to a Stone Temple Pilots concert in the Palms Hotel Show Lounge. He bought the tickets, and we enjoyed a great event. We then later met a girl from Portugal that owned her own business in England. We ran into her and her girlfriends at the main bar of the MGM Casino Hotel. Each guy in there kept warning me to stay away because they had been "working her" for two days and she was just a tease. It appeared she just appreciated someone that treated her like a gentleman should. All I will say is that we really hit it off and she was exactly what I needed to rebound my confidence with a soon-to-be divorce was looming. We hung out all night and most of the rest of the day. We all remained friends for several years after.

The last night we ended up in the Caesar's Palace Hotel. We found the dealers to be the most fun and the atmosphere enticing. This quickly became our go-to place to gamble. We played craps and were on a real hot streak. We were winning so much that The Badger said we needed to head into the High Rollers Room. The stakes were much larger in here with all the chips being at least one hundred dollars and up into the thousands. I was rolling large when a beautiful blonde girl with an Irish accent came right beside me. She kept kissing my dice for good luck before I rolled. I finally hit seven which meant I crapped out. As she was beside me, she was next to roll. She asked the dealer if it was okay to play naked as she had much better luck when playing naked. The pit boss said, "Sure sweetheart. This is Vegas and this room

Chapter 14: The restart of a new life as a bachelor

is private." I could not believe my eyes when she panned it all off. This girl was genetically blessed to say the least. I was trying my best to not stare, as this beauty was someone's daughter. She pulled out thousand-dollar chips and spread them out. Each man threw out our largest chips to try our best to keep up. She now asked me to kiss her hand with the dice for good luck. I mean, I would seriously kiss anything this woman asked me to and especially if anyone is going to get good luck. I already felt like mine was high. She threw the dice across the table then jumped up and down screaming, "Yahoo! I win, I win!" She then grabbed all of the chips off the table and put them into her purse and ran out of the room while putting her dress back on. After we all regained our composure from this stunning display it was the next man's turn to throw the dice. Once we put our new chips on the table, the dealers asked each other if they saw what she had rolled. Neither of the dealers, nor the pit boss, nor any man at the table had a clue. So, the moral of the story is not all blondes are airheads, not all Irish are drunks, but at the end of the day men will always be men! Whether you believe that happened or it's just a bad joke is irrelevant. What happens in Vegas stays in Vegas. All I know is I had to run to find this beautiful woman. After all, I had to find out what she rolled!

The trip to Vegas was just what the doctor ordered, and I felt much better. Once I returned to British Columbia, I picked up a U-Haul. My bags were packed before I left so I planned to drive the U-Haul, pulling my Jeep Cherokee behind it. I later realized that driving a U-Haul with only rear-wheel drive and semi-bald tires through the mountains at the end of the winter was a big mistake. I was coming around hairpin corners with no guard rails. My life was really in the hands of the mountains until I finally got past them. But what a beautiful ride that would be in a proper 4x4 vehicle and having time to enjoy the resort destinations on the Crows Highway.

Before we moved to BC, I had been working on a job opening in the Muskoka's for a couple of years. It was an operations manager position with a one-year growth into the general manager position. It was at The

Taboo Resort. This was a five-star luxury golf resort on the lake. I had gone to three interviews prior to accepting the position at Manning Park in BC. As I did not hear anything back from them, I thought the opportunity had passed. The recruiter representing the position called me and proclaimed this property was owned by a real-estate investment company. The vice president of this corporation was also the acting general manager. He was having such a hard time picking the right candidate because he was replacing himself. I soon realized the operations manager position was already a six-figure salary which would grow into even more in the VP position. This real-estate development company was building condos around the resort area, so the VP was too busy with this to properly manage the resort. I could not believe my ears as to what I was hearing. The recruiter said the VP was flying to BC for a conference and asked to personally see me. Apparently, the VP and recruiter were close friends from working together in the past. He told me, off the record, I would most likely be offered the position as he was staying an extra day to see me. I was thrilled beyond belief.

Before I left for my Las Vegas trip, my aunt in Los Angeles set up a telephone meeting with my father and I to bury the hatchet. My father told me that he and my siblings had made a huge mistake letting me go and asked that I come back to take over the family business. I told him about the opportunity at the resort in Gravenhurst. He said I was passing up the opportunity to own and operate the family business in Sioux Narrows, and I should "just skip that place." He said with all my experience I would be taking over the majority shares as the future president, and they really needed me. He said I would return as the acting general manager of our main lodge property as well as the vice president of all three lodges. He explained this was an even better opportunity for me. It was a very tough decision to turn down the probable offer in southern Ontario, but I felt my family needed me and this was a good opportunity. I packed my U-Haul to head back to northern Ontario.

My wife was extremely upset that I would head back to the family business, as I had worked so hard to be independent. I could not listen to her

Chapter 14: The restart of a new life as a bachelor

as this was the same woman that had just left me for other men. Once I returned home, the divorce with her got very bitter. She threatened to keep my son, as I had lost my custody rights by moving provinces. After much of this for several weeks I was fortunate that her sister lived close to me, so she eventually moved to Kenora so our son could have both parents.

The divorce felt unnecessarily long, and her lawyer seemed to drag it out on purpose. I found a lawyer who drew up an agreement that was fair to both sides. He only asked for a weekend trip to the main lodge for his services. My wife would get enough out of the settlement to pay off her student loans and start out fresh in life. I could not believe that my wife turned this down because her lawyer made an issue out of schooling. I lived in Sioux Narrows, which offered elementary school up to grade six. Kenora is a much larger town, with schooling up to high school. I agreed for my son to be schooled in Kenora grade one to twelve, while taking the bus from Sioux Narrows on my weeks. I felt it was fair for him to do kindergarten in Sioux Narrows and Kenora until grade one started. My wife and her lawyer felt this was too disruptive to his early school development years. I told my wife this lawyer was making an issue to drag out her hourly fees.

My wife insisted on the kindergarten issue to such an extent that junior kindergarten was almost going to be over before we settled. I finally agreed to kindergarten in Kenora. Lo and behold, my wife's lawyer's fees were now so high that she walked away with nothing after our settlement. This is not what I wanted for my son's mother, but things were taken out of my hands. I was also dealt a huge legal fee from my side, so it felt like everyone lost but the divorce lawyers. I am glad we have now moved past all those feelings.

It takes over a year for the Canadian courts to clear a separation into a final divorce agreement. Apparently, this is because many couples change their minds after the smoke clears. I knew I had been betrayed too much to ever go back so we followed the protocol before signing the final papers. With how long it took, it appeared the marriage lasted for several years when it was only about two before she left our residence in BC.

CHAPTER 15:
Back to where it all started.

It took me about a week to drive back from BC to Sioux Narrows. When I arrived, I was put into a cabin we called Wilmarth. This cabin was named for the family that we bought it from. I was told I would be lodging here until I could find reasonable year-round housing for myself. I was also told that food and lodging would always be a part of my compensation package until we worked out the details for me to take over owner's shares.

Moving home started out very well. I was reconnecting with old friends and connecting with girls I did not even know existed. Some of these girls were in their early twenties so I was surprised they even took notice of me at the ripe age of thirty. My father and brother were even coming to my new pad to have beers to welcome me back. Unfortunately, the warm greeting did not last long. As soon as I told the recruiter I was declining the job in southern Ontario and getting myself settled into my cabin, things went back to the negative and toxic energy of the past. I went to the local pub in Sioux Narrows called the Dock House with my brother. The locals were celebrating the fact that I was back. A couple said that the main lodge felt like an empty shell with no soul while I was gone. One fellow asked what my role would be. I really planned to downplay it as just the general manager at the main lodge to get my feet wet and back into the saddle. My brother cut

Chapter 15: Back to where it all started.

me off mid-sentence and said, "He is the boss. He is the GM of everything—so if you need anything with authority, just ask my brother." I instantly realized he was not at all happy to see me back as I could sense his resentment of my position.

My father also changed his tune and said I would need to win back the approval of my siblings. Now that I had left twice, they felt I abandoned the family resort while they had to pick up the extra work loads. It was like the conversations of everyone missing me and learning a lesson in my absence had not even happened. I saw a lot of things had gone wrong while I was away. Long-time employees had either quit or completely disengaged. I could understand why my father wanted me back, as the whole operation had fallen apart. Even though I had not been at any of the resorts to make any decisions on the operations for several seasons, it became my fault for not being there. I could not believe something could be your fault when you were not any part of the planning or execution of it. I was already regretting declining the other offer in southern Ontario. Unfortunately, it was too late, as that ship had now sailed. There is a saying in life that when you make your bed you must lie in it. I decided the honourable thing to do was to honour my commitment to take over as the VP and future president of the resorts. It kind of felt like my obligated family duty. I knew I had the experience and education before I even left, and now I had even more experience. Working at the other operations had taught me things I did not know I needed. Being submissive to other owners was a big growing experience for me.

I ran into my best friend's wife in Kenora, at a pub called Hap's on the harbourfront. This was a well-known pub in the day and tavern in the evenings. Let's call this girl Mrs. Gill, as it was the Rooky's wife. She introduced me to a beautiful young blonde girl and said they needed my assistance. Of course, my first instinct was to help in any way I could. Mrs. Gill informed me that two Frenchmen wanted them to come to their house hot tubbing. She did not feel it was appropriate as she was married and assumed they both wanted her hot blonde friend, and she was just the extra. She asked me to tag along to keep them safe. I knew the two guys would not be happy to see me but I wanted to keep the girls safe. This was also my best chance to get to know her friend.

Mrs. Gill was correct because as soon as we got to the house both guys were all over her friend. They also told us we needed to keep quiet to not waken their family. They said that his parents were visiting but, in the morning, we came to realize he lived with his parents. When I woke up on the couch, everyone had left me, and the parents were upstairs having breakfast. I could tell the father was not happy to see me. I asked for the address and called a taxi to pick me up. As I was looking out the window in the basement, waiting for the taxi, I saw the blonde running out to meet her father who was picking her up. I was hurt and disappointed that she did not offer me a ride and instead ditched me. This young woman and I had really hit it off, as we had snuggled all night on the couch until I woke up. Her family owned two local convenience stores and the *MS Kenora* tourist ship. I knew her parents, as her father was the captain of the ship. He used to organize fish-fry dinner cruises to the island lodge t when I managed it. We had always talked about more business adventures together. Perhaps this young girl was ashamed and did not want her father to think that more than just snuggling happened. As I respect this man very much it was probably the best decision at the time.

Let us call this young girl Ash. This girl was so pretty and ambitious that she was applying for *Playboy*. I felt an instant connection to this girl, so we started dating and really hit it off. I already knew she came from a great family that I had a bond with. She was also smart and ambitious. Most guys might feel it is a personal accomplishment to date a girl who worked for *Playboy* magazine. Lo and behold, this girl's audition was accepted, and she was hired. This meant she had to move to Las Angeles to pursue her modelling career. Unfortunately, this meant our relationship would be short lived. I knew it was best for me to not hold her back, so I came up with other reasons to break up with her. To this day we have remained friends and it is always inspiring

Chapter 15: Back to where it all started.

to watch her modelling career blossom. She has now moved home to take over the family businesses. She is engaged to a nice man, and they have a little son together.

The first year at the resorts was right back to high drama. It took me most of the first year to rebuild the reputation and establish a positive working environment. I was often complimented on getting this done, so I will call it a success. My second summer back was me managing the three operations from our main lodge while my sister managed our boutique lodge, and my brother managed the island lodge. My sister seemed content to stay at the boutique lodge all summer and wanted little to do with the other operations. In the winter, she came into the office to do reservations for this lodge My brother and I went to the sport shows in the winter to market all three resorts. I brought two or three others to help us out. I needed extra help as we manned three booths for three resorts and my brother had little involvement. My brother would usually only come for a couple of hours as he was usually hungover or drinking. This did not offer much help as a salesman.

My second summer back was my first summer of handling all the human resources and hiring for all three resorts. I assumed this role as it gave me the best opportunity to train and mentor the employees. I hired a young girl named Brit to be my brother's personal assistant at the island lodge.

The point of an assistant is to help with day-to-day operations, so the general manager can execute high level duties. Unfortunately, my brother took this as an opportunity to leave the resort frequently and left her in charge of the resort in his absence. As a young girl with no prior resort experience, she was put in a bad position. When my brother returned, his idea of management was to ridicule her for all the things that went wrong. As I could tell this put her in unfair stress, I took it as my obligation to help her. As I had managed the resort for ten years, I still understood it very well. My brother would come back angry and upset at the decisions we had made while he was gone. I angrily explained we should not be making these decisions as it is the responsibility of the GM to be there making them on his own. Unfortunately, my father always defended my brother, so the toxic behaviour grew to be worse. It was obvious that my brother had substance abuse problems, but my father was in denial of this.

As Brit and I ended up working together over the phone, we formed a bond. This bond led to an intimate relationship. It is always a bad idea to date someone you are working with. Quite honestly, I thought she would leave after the summer, and she was only indirectly working for me. After the summer, I grew a deep attachment and feeling for this girl. It made sense, as she grew up coming to Sioux Narrows in the summer visiting family, so felt comfortable there. I would later realize this girl also had a toxic drinking problem.

After the first summer at the island lodge, Brit stayed the winter and helped in the main office. I think she helped with the island lodge reservations, as she knew that operation the best. It always appeared that she was more of an office assistant, as she cleaned the office and did light shores. These chores included answering phone calls, mailing brochures, and very moderate duties. As with my usual winter schedule, I was away at sport shows so did not see her very much. As Brit helped in the office she grew a relationship with the winter reservations coordinator and bookkeeper. It made most sense for her to accept the front office position for the summer season. She was quite skilled at this as she formulated new ideas to sell new- and past-seasons' clothes. She also checked in guests, issued fishing licenses, and insurance forms. After the summer was completed, she stayed into another winter.

Brit had experience in customer service and restaurant service, so we promoted her to the dining room manager position the next summer. As Brit had developed a drinking problem, this would soon become a poor decision both personally and professionally. On a professional level, Brit was drinking leftover wine that customers left on the table after dinner. This caused many dramatic fights between her and the restaurant employees. There was one employee that caused us all many problems. He father brought up a large group in May and was

Chapter 15: Back to where it all started.

debating a return the next season. This server felt she was invincible, as her father spent a lot of money. She quickly caught onto the fact that this was my father's only value. Brit and this young girl fought all summer and caused a huge divide between them and the rest of the employees. As per usual, my father undermined me so we could not discipline this young girl. She laughed at me, saying I held no ground as she worked for my father now. We would later realize this girl's father had moved to a new company and did not have any intention or authority to bring the company back in the future. We were all manipulated.

Brit's drinking also caused me personal problems, as we now lived together. She would come home drunk, yelling at me and proclaiming I did not know how to manage a business. She also proclaimed my whole family was a laughingstock at the resort and in the community. She would get quite violent, throwing things around the house and damaging my property. My young son would lock himself in his room. When he was there, I would take him with me, and when I was by myself, I would leave the house. It was tricky to leave because she would chase me down the road, yelling and screaming. I would wait until she went to the bathroom and sneak out in my truck. I spent many nights sleeping in the backseat of my truck so she could not find me.

I remember calling Brit's parents in the middle of the night. I knew them from visiting at her home in Winnipeg. They were of no help. I think they felt helpless from so far away and were in denial at also being alcoholics—Brit was their only child, so they simply did not want to face the music. Brit's mother had also been diagnosed with breast cancer, so she was on chemotherapy. I can imagine that between the medicine and drinking there was not much energy left to give. My visits told me they were loving and supportive parents, but they just simply could not or would not help with this.

Days led to weeks which led to months and finally a few years. Friends would not consult me anymore as they said I had let this go on for too long. I felt like I was always in a hard place as my family did not not offer support and neither did hers. I was defenseless, as I will not hit a woman even if it's to defend myself, as police informed me is my right. I also felt an obligation to maintain a positive work environment as the leader of the company. I finally got Brit to agree to see a psychologist in Kenora. She claimed he said she did not have a drinking problem. I was not allowed to talk to him to ask, because of doctor-patient confidentiality. He did offer for her to call any time of the day if she was raging with anger, and he would talk her down. I finally got Brit to agree to go back to a dry-out clinic for rehab in Winnipeg, so she could get the alcohol dependency out of her system. I presumed that once I got her away from the lodge, she would sober up and stay in Winnipeg.

When Brit was away, I realized that a past girlfriend was one of my true friends. She realized everything I was going through, so came down with a friend to help me have friendly acquaintances. Another girl that used to work at the lodge was also in the area. Two of my guy friends came, so we coincidentally had three men and three women. It turned out that someone on each side had dated at some point, so we called the boat ride "ex-fest." It was quite comical that we had all remained platonic friends after dating. Nothing romantic happened with any of us but the company sure felt intimate. When Brit returned, she heard about all of us being together and assumed this was some sort of orgy. I quickly realized she did not go to a clinic and had only said she was going to appease me. When Brit came back it somehow got worse.

I went on a cruise with Brit. Her father used to buy vehicles in the USA, keep them for a year or two then sell them. He said it was far less money to buy a vehicle in the States even with the exchange rate. He informed us that you could only purchase one per year without commercial tax, so the government could ensure it was yours. Brit and I bought a used Jaguar in Miami after our cruise for her to have as her own. I paid for ninety percent of the vehicle so we agreed that I would get my money back when she sold it. As soon as we got out of the state of Florida, we realized this car was a lemon. The dealership kept delaying the safety as there was obviously an issue with the starter and recharging assembly. We had to pull into a garage in Tennessee on our

Chapter 15: Back to where it all started.

way home so they could repair it. Once we got home it continued to have more issues. Brit was also chasing me in the middle of the night on her drunken tirades, so she also caused more damage. Her mom laughed and said we never should have bought the colour black, as this was a Jaguar, and black cats are always bad luck.

When the season was over, my father's wife helped pack up Brit's belongings and drove with her back to Winnipeg—her dad met her on the highway. She eventually got a job in Banff, British Columbia. This was three provinces away and with all of her belongings gone, I finally felt safe from the toxicity. I still had the burden of my father and brother but at least this was one less to deal with.

I had an agreement with my father to take over thirty-five percent of the company, with my brother and sister splitting the remainder between them. This gave me the controlling share to make all operation decisions to act as the president and CEO of the company. Each season issues came up for us to not be able to finalize the documents. So even though I acted as the VP, in training to be the president, it never got to his referment. I think that because my father is a manipulator, he always found reasons to put an obstacle in the way

CHAPTER 16:
The day that changed my life forever

Throughout my thirties I lived a life that was in many was like my twenties but was also so different. It was similar in the fact that I was operating a chain of five-star resorts with all the trials and tribulations that come along with it. It was also similar in the challenges I faced in dating women. I can understand the intimidation of dating someone like me, with someone so involved in a highly demanding business. I can also appreciate the difficulties in adapting to such a high-strung and unsupportive family. Girlfriends always tried to show patience and empathy until it finally took an emotional toll on them.

One huge difference in my life has been watching my son grow through all of this. I am pickier in who I allow into his life. His mother will always be his largest female role model but getting serious with a woman is more than just about me. I would ultimately love to have someone by my side who supports me and helps my son in his growing stages. I have come to learn this is a big challenge to find. My son is a gifted athlete who aspires to be a professional baseball player when he grows up. We all have dreams that can sometimes change as we mature. But my son has been exceptional at any sport he plays, with baseball being his biggest passion. He also has a great memory, especially in

Chapter 16: The day that changed my life forever

sports. He remembers the past few years of every athlete for each team that he watches. Even if he does not make it playing on a professional level, there is no doubt his life will always be connected to sports. He has the personality to commentate and the determination to coach or be an agent. He is currently on the local travelling team in the Kenora area called The Selects. There are some amazing coaches that take pleasure in both developing young athletes' skills and organizing the seasons. Our area has always been a hockey town, with that being the primary and almost only focus. It has been great being his biggest fan and attending all of his games. We travel to each city together and he also plays house league as a part of the organization.

Where my life changed was overnight. I invited two of my friends to come and celebrate my fortieth birthday. I had been telling friends all year that my fortieth birthday would be the last time I ever had a drink of alcohol. I exclaimed to my friends they would be the last ones to be with me for such a life-changing occasion.

My Greek friend decided to invite his ex-girlfriend and one of her friends to join us. The plan was to go in my pontoon boat in the day followed by dinner in the main lodge. I was quite excited about my birthday as well as celebrating with two long-time friends, with the chance of meeting two new friends. I remember getting the boat ready. Wild Will was out guiding and said he would meet us later with the Greek and bring both girls to my cabin dock.

I woke up the next morning feeling groggy and confused. I appeared to be in an unfamiliar building that felt quite industrial. As Sioux Narrows is a very small town that I know each inch of, I could not imagine how I ended up in such a strange place. After I woke myself up a nurse came in with a wheelchair and said, "I am so glad you are awake as it is dinner time." I thought this must be a practical joke my friends were playing on me. Was this still my birthday? How much could I have drunk? Or did I get drugged and brought somewhere? The nurse brought me to a dinner table in a small café type area. She explained I was late so no one else was there. She also explained that dinner was at 5 p.m. with no exceptions but that I was hard to wake up. At this point I was looking for cameras, as I had to be getting punked. I was waiting for someone I knew to jump out yelling a birthday surprise and laughing at how I fell for all of this. The nurse had me strapped into the chair and explained I had a difficult time with my balance and walking. I was not at all hungry and had a hard time eating. I also had a hard time getting out of my wheelchair into bed after dinner. I assumed this was a birthday hangover gone bad.

I woke up the next morning and my father was standing beside my bed. I thought, *Yahoo, last night was a dream and I can get up.* I instantly realized I could not stand on my own so sat back down. My father explained that I had been in my side by side with my Greek friend's girlfriend, and we'd had an accident. Apparently, she'd been driving me home and had hit the ditch. She'd done a somersault over the row bar and landed on her feet. I had hit my head against the back row bar and suffered a traumatic brain injury. It was now almost a month past my birthday. Apparently, I had been in a medicinal coma at the HSC in Winnipeg. I was recently brought to the Riverview Rehab Center to help me recover from this accident. I was not happy all of this happened but relieved I finally understood what was going on. My father explained he and his wife had been with me at the hospital every day since my accident.

Thankfully one of the top-ranked surgeons in Canada was on call the night of my accident. He removed a part of my skull so my brain could swell. There were also numerous operations performed on me while I was asleep. Riverview is considered one of the top-ranked brain repair hospitals in the world, so we were just lucky to live close enough to it. A doctor came into my room explaining I was a miraculous miracle of life. This injury would have killed ninety-five percent of people. While I was in there, I also got pneumonia, so a trace was put into my neck. I had a custom-built hockey helmet on my head to protect me. I also had a tube in my belly to give me the proper nourishment, as I could not eat.

Chapter 16: The day that changed my life forever

This all happened in the summer of 2016. That winter I was 230 lbs and slimmed down to 215 lbs. I had always been an athletic person and had completed six half marathons. The doctors said the conditioning was what saved my life as I had the heart rate of an Olympic athlete. I was now only weighing 160 lbs. I lost a lot of weight during the time in the emergency rooms. Aside from my brain injury, I also had liver damage from the medicines they had to give me while in operations. I could barely eat, due to my stomach and intestines both shrinking.

I felt fine to talk and communicate which seemed to surprise most people. I was a little annoyed at everyone treating me with childlike gloves and talking down to me. I can appreciate that everyone handles distress in their own way. My ego was offended at how low everyone viewed my chances. I decided to use this as my own personal motivation.

One story I remember is a girl coming into my hospital room. I hired her mid-season from one of my fishing guides telling me she needed a break from the city. We called this girl Skinny Nicky as she was extremely thin. She came into my room and jumped into my bed as though we were in an intimate relationship. Even though I had hired this girl, I barely knew her as she was only there a couple of weeks before my accident. My father winked and gave me a thumbs up while he and his wife left. This was all extremely awkward. She asked if I hated her, to which I replied, "No. I have a new lease on life and feel God gave me a second chance." She explained that on the night of my accident she had asked me to ditch my friend so she and I could go up to her room to knock her up—apparently my Greek friend's girlfriend had heard this, so took me on the side by side to help me escape this. Skinny Nicky explained she had watched the side by side the whole way. She now propositioned me to knock her up in the hospital. The lights in the hallway flickered so I told her visiting time was over and asked security not to allow her back in. The emotions of being flattered and scared ran through me … but more scared.

To say the least, I could not believe how much my life had changed in the time I woke up. Riverview assessed I would be in this hospital for a minimum of two to three and maybe four years. They could not believe I got out in three months. I was determined to live back on my own. They released me as an outpatient and referred me to many specialists in my areas: Occupational Therapy, Speech Therapy, Physiotherapy. I had all kinds of names I had never heard before. I was also having seizures, so I lost my driver's license for almost two years until the cognitive doctors could figure it all out.

The brain surgeon that saved my life brought me back in to have my skull bone put back in place. Apparently, they kept it frozen until I was ready to have it screwed back in. He explained that some things in my life would change. I would no longer be able to drink alcohol or caffeine and permanent retirement was mandatory. He said, "Congratulations, you are retired at forty." Because of this diagnosis, I was issued disability insurance and CPP Disability Insurance helped me sustain my life financially. I was okay with not drinking alcohol as I had planned not to anyway. Learning to retire unexpectedly, at such a young age, has been an adjustment.

My father told me that I am a financial burden to the resort and an operation distraction to my siblings who had to assume my positions. I now reside in my own home in Kenora with my son. I continue split custody of him and will until he has graduated from high school.

Final Closing Thoughts:

I would like to thank everyone that was a part of my life and for making it worth putting into words through a novel. The good, the bad, the ups and downs are all a part of sculpting us into who we are created to be. I hope that anyone that I put in here can take it as a compliment—that they helped me become the man that stands here today. I have had many positive and inspirational influences that have taught me lessons of strength, gratitude, and humbleness. I have also learned from the negative impacts of people who may have worries, fears, and regrets that live deep within them. Everyone has something to teach, whether it is intended or merely happens by accident.

    I hope that those who were not mentioned do not take this as an insult or feel forgotten and insignificant. It is best to respect the privacy of those we know prefer to be left alone. Introverts prefer to be left alone to observe and watch the energies around them … but just know that you are still with us. Extroverts prefer to be a part of the party and potential chaos around them. I hope that we can live in a world that embraces each other's differences instead of mocking them. We need not be judged by our race, colour, sexual preferences, religion, or political backgrounds. We are all unique and beautiful in our own ways.

    Thank you to all the heroes of the world. The heroes that fight in battle to keep us safe. The heroes that stand up for things they believe in and making the world a better place to live in. Thank you to the mothers that carry a baby in their womb while it grows inside of them, then make sacrifices to their bodies to make sure that child is healthy. Thank you to all of the parents, relatives, educators, coaches and mentors that influence our children to be the future of mankind. Thank you to anyone who has ever disagreed with me to show me I am not always right. Thank you to anyone who has doubted me—this challenged me to prove you wrong. It is the doubters that challenge us to improve ourselves. Thank you to the hardest working people who do not do it for the rewards but because it needs to be done the best it can be. You all have taught me so much in my life. I hope I can be as great at passing on inspiration to those around me, as I strive to have a more positive influence on anyone I have touched in my life.

Thank you to my son who is a much better and more positive image of me. You make it look easy to be a parent with your hard work, determination, grace, and manners. You make the world a better place for anyone you are around. Thank you to his mother who helps me raise him—your love and devotion surely has a great impact on him. Even though we are no longer together, thank you for believing I was worth marrying and spawning a beautiful child with. Thank you to his stepfather and sister who are a big part in completing his loving home while he's with you.

Thank you to everyone that reads this book ... Yes, that means you who is reading it now. Thank you for taking the time to share my memories with me. I have not written a sequel as I still have a lot of life to live and memories to make. So that is yet to be written in the future. I look forward to anyone that comes into my future journeys!

Most importantly, thank you to our Lord and Saviour for providing us with such a great planet to live in. Thank you for giving me the wisdom, strength, and courage to battle my daily, weekly, monthly, and yearly challenges. Thank you for forgiving us our sins and providing us with warmth, shelter, food, and nourishment to fuel our bodies while here on your earth. May God bless everyone in this beautiful world.

Printed in Canada